Freedom Is

Freedom Is

Liberating Your Boundless Potential

BRANDON BAYS

First published in Great Britain in 2006 by Hodder & Stoughton
A division of Hodder Headline

A Mobius Book

1

A CIP catalogue record for this title
is available from the British Library

0 340 92100 5

Typeset in Optima by Hewer Text UK Ltd, Edinburgh
Printed and bound by Clays Ltd, St Ives plc

Hodder Headline's policy is to use papers that are natural, renewable
and recyclable products and made from wood grown in sustainable
forests. The logging and manufacturing processes are expected to
conform to the environmental regulations of the country of origin.

Hodder & Stoughton Ltd
A division of Hodder Headline
338 Euston Road
London NW1 3BH

In gratitude to the
Infinite Grace
pervading all of life

Contents

Introduction 1

1. Effortless Being 7
2. Non-attachment 31
3. Present-moment Awareness 55
4. Honouring and Reverence 81
5. Emotions 105
6. Gratitude 139
7. Love 167
8. Forgiveness 195
9. Enlightenment 225

introduction

This book is written to give you a *living* experience of freedom. It is a powerful call from deep within you to come home to the boundless presence of grace that is always here. It is not designed as a quick read where you simply collect yet more knowledge or anecdotal titbits. Rather, it is meant to provide you with a sublime *experience* of the infinite. It is an invitation to relax, become still and open deeply into a wordless presence that is here in the spaces *between* the words. If you stop now . . . pause . . . grow still, you will sense a strong presence pulling you into yourself, into the wordless wisdom already here. This presence is your own essence. It is vast, free and completely whole. It is a huge unborn potential; full of creativity, genius, wisdom – capable of creating anything. It is alive with grace, always here and continuously available. This book provides you with a natural, effortless opening into this exquisite presence, and it gives you the means to clear anything that might obscure your experience of it – in very real, practical and accessible ways.

This is not a book *about* freedom. This is a book that draws you *into* it, into the infinite, into the boundless presence of your own inner being.

As you read this book let it be experiential. Drink in the words, savour them, let them seduce you and reverberate through your whole being. Take time to bask in the stillness inherent in the spaces *between* the sentences. The stillness there is calling you into the embrace of the infinite. It is calling you right now. Stop . . . breathe . . . listen with your being. This calling is completely familiar to you. It is already known. Your own essence is calling you home.

✡ ✡ ✡

Each chapter is designed to carry you deeply into a different aspect of your essence. Though in truth there is no *one* specific word that can describe this boundless presence, there are various qualities that seem to arise from it. As with a rose, even though the fragrance that emanates from it is not the rose itself, so it is with these various aspects of grace. Though grace is wordless, timeless, infinite, and cannot be defined by any one single characteristic, still this presence exudes particular fragrances. The invitation here is to let go and fall into the fragrance of each chapter, letting freedom embrace you in its beauty and allowing a deep teaching to arise effortlessly from within.

Following each teaching will be a guided meditation, introspection, process or contemplation designed to help you open even further – to draw you directly and experientially into the vast embrace. Some of the process work is in-depth, whereas other contemplations will take only a few minutes. Each and every tool will continue to work on your inner being throughout your day, and will cause you to feel a greater level of peace and connection with yourself and others in your life.

The work is practical, useable and can be introduced into your everyday life gracefully and effortlessly.

Once you've fully experienced the book in its entirety, you might like to begin a daily practice. You can open the book randomly, let your awareness rest on the page and ask to be guided from within. As you read, let your awareness be relaxed and spacious: listen *beyond* the words and allow them to do their work, letting yourself fall into the vast embrace of that particular quality of your own essence. As you open, your own deeper wisdom will begin to reveal itself naturally.

As you begin to let this book work on you and transform your life, it will become a living, breathing teaching. You might like to spend fifteen minutes each day and view it as quiet time spent with yourself, letting your inner wisdom reveal new lessons and deeper teachings each time you open it anew. Sometimes as you read a paragraph and pause to let it seep in, your own truth will reveal just how that quality is currently present in your life. Or you might spontaneously experience how it could help heal or resolve a specific situation. Sometimes, as the words settle into your being, you will feel a profound stillness suffused with a crystal clarity, which might have a purposeful, directive quality to it, and you will feel a strong inner guidance. If you feel called to, you can go to the end of the chapter and undergo the in-depth exploration or discovery process to deepen your experience and realisation.

Each time you open into your own essence will be the first time, for grace is always fresh, always new. Even if you've already dived in and experienced the whole book from cover to cover, each time you open it, the book will reveal something unexpected, something different. Somehow, what arises will be synchronistically perfect for that moment.

No meditation, introspection or contemplation is ever the same, and, as you open into them in all innocence and trust yourself, deeper and more profound wisdom will be revealed. Sometimes this realisation will come in words, and sometimes it will reveal itself wordlessly, as a deep inner knowing.

As you learn to open more freely and trust more completely, this book may become a dear friend or spiritual companion calling you back home to yourself, inviting you to experience the embrace of grace that is always here. This book is an adventure, a journey in the truest sense: full of revelations, experiences of the infinite, and clearing process work with deep guided meditations and profoundly opening contemplations. It is chock-full of inspiring stories that will continually evoke deeper understanding, and practical, useable techniques that can be applied in all areas of your life.

Ultimately, this book is designed to transform your life into one of effortless ease filled with grace and joy. It teaches you how to apply your own wisdom to everyday situations in very real and simple ways. And it gives you the tools to live your life in gratitude, love and freedom.

This book truly is a journey within yourself – into the boundless presence of freedom that is what you are.

May you fall in love with this presence, and may the exquisite embrace of grace seduce you ever deeper.

effortless being

Effortless being is the sublime presence
that suffuses all fragrances of grace.
It is whole, free and completely at ease –
and it requires nothing.

Just let yourself relax . . . trust . . . open . . .
and gracefully fall into effortless being.

It seems appropriate to begin our journey together with effortless being, as it is the one quality of grace that is intrinsic to and inherent in all aspects of the infinite. Any time you open into the infinite presence of your own self, an effortless presence will have easily and gracefully guided you there. In fact, the only route I know of into enlightened awareness is through effortless being.

So why not plunge in right now? Rather than talk about it, let's experience it directly.

Take a deep breath in, and let it out. And another deep breath in, and let it out. Let your whole being relax as you fully put yourself into this scene and experience it as if it is actually happening right now. Take time in between the sentences to open and *feel* what it is really like to be in these circumstances. Just imagine what it would be like if *you* were the person featured in this story . . .

> You are in the ocean, out of your depth, struggling to stay afloat. The more you struggle the less buoyant you feel. Each effort feels more and more exhausting. Fighting what is, you believe the answer lies in trying harder . . . reaching, grasping with your whole being, striving with your body, harnessing your mind, trying to focus all of your energy to stay

above water, you fight for your life. Your activity becomes frenetic. A sinking futility starts to creep in but you realise you can't give in, no matter what. You force your mind into high gear. You struggle with all your might. Your striving becomes frantic.

A kind person throws you a life preserver, but it lands just of your reach. Safety is but a few feet away, if only you could grasp it in time. Certain that effort is the only answer, you harness every fibre of your being, desperately trying to grasp the answer to all your prayers . . . knowing that all peace, all rest, life itself is just an arm's length away, just out of reach . . . if only you try harder, the prize of freedom, relaxation, safety will be yours.

But with each fiercely desperate stroke, you end up pushing the life preserver further away. The fight intensifies. You feel your mind is starting to spin out of control. You force it into line . . . everything depends on this final struggle to win, but your very striving is driving it further . . . and further . . . and further away.

Finally, the kind stranger jumps into the water, and when he bobs to the surface all movement ceases. He is just floating. He appears motionless . . . as if he is just resting, simply trusting. Gently, under the surface, his legs are flowing in the quietest of movements; effortlessly treading water, trusting completely in the ease of Grace. The water becomes still and the life preserver, which is no longer being pushed away by the thrashing around, is free to drift his way . . . Resting . . . trusting . . . relaxing . . . lap . . . by lap . . . by lap . . . the life preserver finds its way into his hands, and with almost no movement, more a softly whispered prayer than an actual motion, he glides it your way.

You frantically grasp for it and, once again, it drifts just out of your reach. The desperation becomes unbearable.

You hear a reassuring voice say, 'RELAX . . . Just RELAX . . . you're safe . . . Trust . . . All safety is here . . . everything you need is *already* here'. Then, once again, the kind man who trusts the ocean, trusts life, trusts grace, softly floats the life preserver in your direction.

It is only one arm's length away. The desire to reach for it is fiercely strong. The impulse to grasp arises. 'One last struggle and I'm there', you hear yourself say, but before you can thrust out your hand, you hear the stranger say again, 'JUST RELAX.'

And something penetrates . . . it happens in a heartbeat. Against all instincts, against all ingrained beliefs and all societal conditioning, against everything you've ever held to be true, you decide to do the impossible. You *choose to cease striving* . . . You relax. You relax your mind . . . you give up all struggle and relax your whole being. You feel your body softening and, miraculously, the life preserver begins to effortlessly drift your way.

Just before it's ready to softly touch your chest, *something happens.* Time stops . . . everything becomes still . . . Your breathing slows down and becomes easy . . . The contraction of your mind softens and every ounce of activity ceases. Your body releases all tension and you become aware that you are being softly supported, embraced in an ocean of trust . . . In the still centre of the silence, you realise that all grace is here, surrounding you, supporting you. All peace is here, all rest is here . . . And you relax deeply in the restful embrace of grace . . .

You become aware that the life preserver has just tapped you on the chest . . . and in that instant you realise that you don't actually need it, you *never* needed it. You're already safe, already whole, already free. You're floating in an ocean of trust. Life preserver, no life preserver . . . same, same.

Gently, one arm floats to the side of the preserver, and you look around to see if there is anyone else struggling needlessly in the water . . . And *you* become the kind stranger.

A soft smile of irony creeps across your face as you realise the ludicrous insanity of struggling against life. It's like some big cosmic joke. Everything you had been seeking is recognised to be already here the moment you *chose to stop the struggle, relax and trust.* This that had seemed so far out of reach is realised to be everywhere, in everything. And that 'something out there, if only I could get hold of it,' is realised to be *right here,* as a vast embrace, constantly supporting you in an ocean of presence.

And so it is with grace. The more you struggle, strive, fight, reach, grasp or force your mind, the further away you push the very peace you are seeking. And the moment you stop, soften the mind, relax your body, cease striving, *give up the struggle,* the peace you are seeking is directly experienced to be here as a spacious presence of effortless being.

The very nature of grace is effortless ease. It is already completely complete, whole, free, vast and open. It intrinsically knows how to care for every aspect of your life, and it is always in flow. Like a river flowing over water-smoothed rocks, it has a natural ease. Yet it's as if there is no one doing the doing, or 'flowing the flow'. It just *is*. It is simultaneously supremely restful and scintillatingly alive: it loves to give birth to creation. It is as if this flow knows the right action in each moment. There is no 'somebody' there controlling, managing and directing its natural momentum. With effortless ease it flows through life.

As children, so often we heard, '*Try* to do your best.' And our focus went to the *trying*. We struggled, we strived, we fought. Had we instead been told, 'Relax little one – you are already whole and perfect, and there is a huge potential that is longing to create through you – just relax,' we *would* have relaxed, opened and allowed our genius, creativity and love to shine. We would have just opened innocently and allowed our wisdom to arise naturally, and would have been delighted to simply be part of the process of creation.

Unfortunately, most of us became conditioned to the idea that struggling is good and makes us strong, and we feel guilty if we take even a few spare moments to relax. But ironically, it is only when you completely let go into full relaxation that true genius and creativity become available.

Have you ever tried to remember someone's name and felt that the word was just on the edge of your awareness, if only you could grasp it? And no matter how hard you tried, you just couldn't come up with the name? Then do you remember what happened? How you *gave up the struggle, relaxed,* stopped reaching with the mind, and moments later, when the mind was totally at ease, the name just popped into your awareness.

So it is with grace. If you force yourself to meditate, setting your mind into a certain groove, focusing on an object, concentrating and repeating mantras, your very efforting keeps away the peace you are seeking. Yet when you just relax, become aware of all sounds, have no purpose other than to close your eyes and 'just be', not caring whether thoughts come or go through consciousness, letting yourself naturally glide into a spacious awareness, you find yourself soaking deeply in a restful ocean of healing presence. Then, when thoughts come through, you realise that the stillness is untouched by anything that comes through it.

The moment you grasp or grab onto a thought and try to interpret it, understand its significance, all awareness of the ocean drops into the background and your whole being goes to the thought. It's only when you *choose to stop reaching* to analyse the constructs of the mind that you find yourself falling again, back into the ocean – the ocean of effortless being. *All* struggle, striving, efforting only takes you away. *All* letting go, opening, accepting, trusting allows you to fall deeper and deeper into the embrace.

Cease all activity and just rest.

Any effort made in meditation just pushes grace away. Indeed, this is true of all life.

I remember once, I was working with my grandfather in his workshop. Grandpa had a PhD in physics, and loved to invent things and work with his hands, crafting his own creations, bringing them into physical form.

When I was twenty-three, I had an idea that I wanted to make a very special Christmas present for my husband. He loved the game of backgammon, and so I went to Grandpa and explained my vision: that I had bought some gorgeous fabric from Liberty in London, and I wanted to build a backgammon set that would allow the beauty of the cloth to be seen. I would have liked to make a glass box but as that was virtually impossible to manufacture, not to mention impractical to use, I decided to use transparent Perspex. Grandpa always loved a challenge, and began to research the various types, thicknesses and properties of Perspex.

After all his findings, he came up with a special brittle version that wouldn't crack or scratch as easily as other types, but he warned me it would have to be handled 'with kid gloves'.

We spent an afternoon together designing it, figuring out how the joints could marry up together and actually bond into something strong and useable, and finally, when the special order Perspex arrived, we went down to his workshop to begin constructing our complex, but well-thought-out box.

Grandpa began bending the Perspex, checking its flexibility and its brittleness – where the breaking point was. From his vast experience of building and crafting, he had selected and laid out three specific sawing implements that might penetrate the material (though he had to admit that laser cutting, sadly unavailable, would have given us the finest edge). After several breaks and misapplied pressure, he scored a perfect line, then gently slotted in his saw, creating the finest of grooves, and perfectly cleaved off the remaining piece.

It *looked* so easy.

Not wanting to make me feel self-conscious, he casually said, 'OK, I'll leave you to it and go upstairs to see how your grandmother is getting on.'

Carefully, I scored the edge, and slowly I lifted the cutting saw. Like Grandpa, I tried to gain purchase with the right angle, but 'snap', the Perspex cracked in two.

I took a deep breath in. Perspex of this type was expensive, hard to get, and had to be specially ordered. 'OK, this time I'll try harder. This time I need to focus my mind, steady my hand,' I willed myself to get it right. I had all the right intentions. 'I will do it right this time,' I kept repeating in my head.

I held my breath. I scored the Perspex. I steadied my hand and began to saw. It wasn't working. I pushed harder. It *had* to work.

Snap! The next piece of Perspex broke in two.

Tears welled in my eyes. I couldn't afford to lose another piece. I mustered all my concentration, all my will. I summoned all focus, and once again, Snap!

My head started spinning. Hot tears streamed down my cheeks. I wiped them with the sleeve of my shirt, and with a red nose and a set jaw went upstairs to Grandpa and admitted that I'd blown it. I just couldn't get it right, no matter how *hard* I tried.

Grandpa, having met frustration many times in his life, smiled reassuringly. 'It's only plastic dear. We can order some more.'

'But Grandpa, you made it look so easy.'

'Well why don't we go back down to the workshop and see what we can cobble together? Maybe I can melt the Perspex with my torch, get some bonding glue, pumice it, sand it, buff and glue it. Perhaps the crack won't even show. Let's see.'

We went downstairs and he looked at my botch job and said, 'Show me how you're cutting it, dear.'

I scored a clean piece, gained purchase with my saw, and just as I began to work it, it snapped – broken in two again.

Grandpa said, 'Brandon, look me in the eyes. Do you see how quiet I become *before* I even pick up an instrument? Now, look how it floats in my hand. You need to think of this saw as if it's a feather that you're stroking through water . . . softly, easily, effortlessly . . . Like this.'

This burly mountain of a man delicately held the saw, as if it was made of air. He scored a piece with the lightness of a gentle caress. The saw began to glide gracefully through the plastic. It looked impossible, but the less effort he used the deeper and freer his movement was. He took my hand and held it, as if holding a small bird. 'Like this Brandon . . . Less is more . . . Just let it slide . . . No pushing, striving . . . Just let it find its own way. Let the Perspex *teach you* how deep, how fast.'

And so it did. And an exquisite Perspex cabinet box brought itself into being, as I effortlessly surrendered into letting *it* teach me.

It's now nearly 30 years since I first opened and discovered the power of effortless being with my grandfather, and in all this time I've never seen a more beautiful backgammon board – ever.

✡ ✡ ✡

The power and presence of effortless being actually revealed itself much earlier in life. I frequently had glimpses or tastes, but they were fleeting and mostly passed through awareness unrecognised. Then, when I was twenty-two years old, I had a very strong taste. I was newly married, and as a wedding gift, my husband gave me the realisation of one of my personal dreams. For our first honeymoon night he bought us hugely coveted box seat tickets to a purportedly spectacular performance of the ballet *Romeo and Juliet* at the Metropolitan Opera in New York City. Rudolph Nureyev was the featured performer, and people had purchased their tickets up to six months and more prior, to score a prized seat at what was to be an extraordinary event.

I will never forget that night for as long as I live. It was pure magic. There came a moment where an unexpected opening into grace took place. Rudolph, who had been dancing sublimely, taking our breath away throughout the night, appeared to be in a flow of grace that was exquisite. Then, during one of his solos, something unexplainable happened. He seemed to be falling into some glorious reverie as he was spinning, turning, pirouetting across the vast open stage. Just as he was preparing to leap into the air, *time stopped* for a fraction of a second . . . We all felt it and drew a deep breath in together. In that moment, where everything came to a complete standstill, it seemed as if Rudolph was letting go of all his hard-earned skill and expertise. Like a great, invisible mantle, it all fell away . . . it was palpable. And when he leapt into the air it was as if somehow he had been set entirely free: free to soar like a bird. His strong, athletic body seemed to be made of air. He'd completely abandoned himself into an effortless grace. As he leapt, he seemed to float for an instant, and then the impossible happened. His legs reached out, as if expanding like wings, and somehow he lifted infinitesimally higher into the air.

Everyone gasped; our hair stood on end as a wave of unfathomable but palpable realisation wafted as a thrill through the audience. The leap seemed to go on endlessly – it seemed timeless.

Wordlessly, we all experienced it together. One person had effortlessly completely opened into infinite being, and we *all* caught it. We felt it ripple through. We tasted the opening.

At the end of his performance the hall became a din of endless cheering, applauding, faces streaming with tears. We could not seem to find an adequate way to express our gratitude. We were bursting with joy and our tribute went on for forty-five minutes – all because we'd been given just a taste of effortless grace.

Truly, it's when we put aside all of our knowing, all of our conditioning, all of our hard work, and cast off all that we *think* we've learned, that effortless being is revealed. When we courageously throw off our whole invisible mantle of 'the known' – and it's a heavy mantle to carry – that is when we fall innocently into effortless being.

Effortless grace is always here, always available, always surrounding and infusing you. Indeed, it is your very essence. And it is easily revealed when you choose to let go of your ideas of how things *should* be, and just open into the innocence of the unknown.

And from this effortless being, true genius is born, and magic happens.

✲ ✲ ✲

My father had a different kind of genius to Rudolph. As a scientist and engineer, his genius lay in inventing incredibly complex radar systems. During the 60s and into the 70s he worked for the US defence department, and his brief was to design and oversee the building of radars that would alert us to possible attack from foreign missiles. He was designing mind-bogglingly complicated systems to help protect the American people, and felt weighed down, practically crushed by the responsibility he shouldered.

As he was the inventor and the designer, no one else had his expertise and understanding of the intricacies of the designs, so if something went wrong in either the conceptual or the building phase, only he had the knowledge to fix it. Carrying all the weight of that responsibility, he would stay up until all hours of the night, poring over calculations on the 400-plus page data sheets that the cumbersome think-tank computers had spat out. When there was an error, the computer couldn't find it – it was up to him.

At 4:00 a.m. one night the strain and anxiety became too much. He couldn't find the error, couldn't figure out the answer. Somewhere in those 400-odd pages of data something was wrong but, like a needle in a haystack, it seemed impossible to find.

In despair he went to bed, and before he fell asleep he simply *gave up* altogether. All he could muster was to put out what seemed like an impossibly futile prayer that somehow the solution would be revealed in the morning. Being a highly practical, logical, analytical man, this seemed like a ludicrous request, but it was his last thought before he fell into a short and fitful night's sleep.

At 6:45 a.m. bleary-eyed, my dad opened his eyes and, as he reached to turn off the alarm, both the mistake and the perfect solution suddenly appeared in his consciousness.

He jumped out of bed, tore through the tall stack of data pages and found it. There was the error, sticking out like a sore thumb. By 8:00 a.m. the formula was corrected and the correct calculations worked out. He went to work with a solution in his hand, triumphant that his team of several hundred men could continue to build the radar.

That same night at dinner, Dad shared his revelation with all the family. It was when all of his knowledge, learning, background, even his analytically astute genius was put aside that an answer became effortlessly available from some deep place in consciousness. When all striving ceased, all anxiety was finished, then an answer became obviously apparent.

When I think of the countless sleepless nights my dad suffered, I dearly wish he'd discovered this secret sooner. And I wish, after such an astounding revelation, that he'd remembered it more often. He made life so hard for himself.

But, like my dad, most of us are conditioned to trust our minds and our thought processes, even when we've had a taste of something deeper. We've come to worship the thoughts coming through awareness, believing them to be real, instead of trusting something *deeper* than our minds, something that only arises in thought-free awareness – grace.

Finding true answers simply requires that we give up the arrogant belief that our minds have the answers and are in control. It's when we let go into the infinite that grace can use our minds as neutral vehicles that transmit knowledge born from the timeless, eternal presence.

Albert Einstein understood this simple principle. In order to access true genius and formulate the theories that would transform the way the whole world perceived the universe, he openly shared that he would close his eyes, become still and, 'go into the still, dark place where God is.' Though he didn't use our words, his actions were those of one who understood the power of the infinite. Grace was giving rise to all genius, all creativity, all answers. His only job was to close his eyes and effortlessly fall in.

Effortless being is the key that unlocks the wisdom of the universe. And it has always been here, always will be, and is always available once *you choose to give up the struggle*.

✲ ✲ ✲

Over the years I've fallen in love with this effortless grace. And whenever the impulse arises to effort or struggle, I instantly grow suspicious of it. I *know*, absolutely *know* in every fibre of my being, that grace is whole, complete, requires nothing, needs nothing, and certainly does *not* need *my* help or efforting. So the only one who could possibly feel the desire to struggle would be ego itself. And these days, if any tendency to effort arises, I stop instantly, recognise ego is trying to take charge of something or control something, and I know that any effort whatsoever will stop the easy flow of grace.

Around The Journey, our seminars organisation, so much manifests in a single year – so many countries are visited, thousands of lives are utterly transformed – that when we look back at all that has taken place in a particular year, we realise that it is equivalent to what should have been accomplished over maybe five years! That can only be the flow of grace in action. Even the entire Journey team could not have manifested and accomplished the abundance and richness of results that grace was able to create. It always blows me away to look back and recognise the variety of miracles grace has blessed us with.

So, I'm acutely watchful now: if even a whisper of efforting arises, I instantly realise that it might get in the way of the magical flow of grace that is perfectly manifesting and orchestrating everything around me, and I stop everything . . . I close my eyes, I *choose* acceptance and trust, and I fall into effortless being. Then I pray that grace will reveal the highest action in the right time, and I surrender to letting the divine take the helm and guide the way.

I often joke with people that grace has me tethered on a leash – I innocently follow along, and go where I'm guided. Then, when all the extraordinary healing, transformation, realisation, liberation and joy is manifesting around me, I know that grace has been in charge. Only the infinite could be responsible for such magnificence. All credit belongs to grace.

For me to take charge, assume control or take credit for the bountiful miracle of grace's manifestation would be as ridiculous as a twig carried by a torrential river to the ocean taking credit for getting there.

The river of grace is all knowing, all pervasive, unavoidable, relentless, and there is no other choice for me than to surrender, trust and relax into the infinite.

I pray that you will fall so in love with this effortless ease that any impulse to struggle will become an immediate invitation to relax, open and accept.

Guided Introspection – Effortless Being

Are there ways you've been efforting lately? Have you railed against something that is just the way things are? Have you fought against what is or tried to make things go *your* way, feeling like you're forcing a square peg into a round hole?

Are you fed up with this fruitless and insane game? And are you ready to give up fighting your paper tigers, and give in to effortless ease? Then you're ready for a guided introspection. There are a number of ways you can do this process: If you have bought the companion CD for this book, you should use it for this Introspection. If not, you could record your own voice reading out the passage below, and play it back to yourself with closed eyes; or you could ask a friend to sit with you, and from a place of openness, softly read it to you. Alternatively you could just start by taking in some slow, deep breaths, keeping your consciousness soft and spacious, and read it as an open-eyed meditation allowing the words to carry you deep within.

So, take a nice deep breath in . . . and let it out . . . Another long, slow breath in . . . and let it gracefully flow out . . . Another long, easy breath in . . . and slowly breathe it out.

Now, let your awareness begin to open out spaciously in front . . . let it become open and vast behind . . . feel it expanding spaciously to all sides . . . Notice the vastness below . . . and the boundless sky above . . . and just rest now, as open spaciousness . . . as a vast, open embrace of stillness . . . just rest.

Now, in a relaxed way, scan your body with your awareness . . . There are probably some areas that are more tense than the rest . . . Go to an area where there is a bit of tension and, for a moment, make it even more tense, more tight . . . increase the resistance . . . Now, release it all at once . . . Breathe into it and feel your breath dissolving any residual tension . . . Keep breathing long, slow breaths as it continues to dissolve.

Now find another area of tension . . . Intensify, or contract that area . . . and breathe it out, all at once . . . Feel it releasing . . . Surround it with your awareness . . . Breathe in spaciousness . . . and release the breath into that area, as the tension continues to dissolve with the out breath.

Keep contracting and releasing until all of your body feels fully relaxed and open.

Now, check your mind . . . Feel your mind closing like a fist . . . clamping down, contracting, resisting . . . And now, with the out breath, blow the tension out . . . feel it relaxing, softening, easing . . . Breathe spaciousness in . . . and breathe warmth and ease out . . . Let the tension of the mind relax completely . . . continuing to dissolve with the breath.

Now check your being . . . If there is any holding on, or fighting with life, or resistance to what is, intensify it for a moment . . . And then sigh it out . . . Feel your being relaxing . . . Continue to release as you sigh it out.

Once again, allowing all the relaxation to spread . . . becoming vast in front . . . free and open behind . . . spacious and expansive to all sides . . . infinite below . . . and spacious and open above . . . just rest now . . . as an ocean of relaxing presence . . . deeply vast.

Now welcome into your awareness something that you've been efforting with, or fighting against lately . . . Welcome yourself to fully *feel* the tension and contraction you feel when you are fighting with what is . . . Like the person in the ocean fighting for his or her life, feel the intensity and futility of trying to struggle and resist life . . . Feel how it affects your body . . . your mind . . . your being . . . Be willing to feel it become even more intense . . . Fight harder, create more resistance . . . Effort with all your might.

Now, what if you discovered that everything *is as it is meant to be*? . . . What if you realised that everything that is taking place is happening for a reason and a purpose that you can't fully understand yet? . . . What if you were to fully, completely and utterly *just accept what's here*?

What if it is entirely the will of grace, and is out of your hands? . . . What if there is nothing you can do, should do, or ought to do to fix it? . . . What if you finally felt what it feels like to completely and totally *relax and accept* that what is here is what is meant to be, in this moment?

What if, in absolutely accepting, you chose now to *stop struggling* . . . *give up* . . . *relax* . . . just relax . . . let go?

What if, as you let go, you felt yourself deeply releasing, falling, opening, relaxing into a spacious embrace of infinite presence? . . . What if this presence was surrounding you, suffusing you . . . pulling you ever deeper . . . opening . . . relaxing . . . *trusting* . . . *trusting* . . . *trusting*?

How would it feel to rest in an ocean of trust . . . just being . . . effortless being?

What if you gave up the need to figure it out, find the answers, fix it, change it, make it right? . . . What if you just *accepted totally* . . . that what is here is what is here?

Just relax in the infinite embrace of pure being . . . No action needed . . . no agenda . . . no desire . . . no grasping for understanding.

Just this . . . just this that is here in the abundance of all that is.

And what if you had full permission just to rest, and effortlessly not know anything? . . . How would that feel?

Just rest, soak, steep in effortless grace for the next few moments.

With nothing to gain, learn, achieve or change, ask, 'If grace were to take care of this problem, situation, circumstance, how might it get handled easily, effortlessly?'

And let the question go . . . Let it go completely . . . and leave the answer up to grace to reveal in its mysterious way . . . with its divine timing . . . when it is ready to.

And then, if you are to be used as a vehicle by grace as a part of some action or solution, the result is not up to you . . . it's up to grace . . . No doer . . . No agenda . . . No credit taking . . . just non-personal guidedness.

Leave it in the hands of grace. If you're needed to play some part, it will happen effortlessly.

If you feel efforting arising at *any* time, internally say, '*Stop.*' Cease struggling, relax your body and let grace get on with what it knows how to do perfectly.

Take a nice, deep breath in . . . and let it out . . . another nice deep breath in . . . and let it out.

And if your eyes have fallen closed, you may open them now.

non-attachment

When the strings of attachment loosen,
dissolve and float away
you are left soaring in freedom
on the wings of grace.

I learned a lesson in non-attachment that forever changed my relationship to the outer 'things' in my life – my possessions, my home, my relationships, my lifestyle, even my own body.

About fifteen years ago, I was sitting in a meditation retreat with Gurumayi, an enlightened master who often teaches in the traditional manner through powerful stories. This particular story really impacted me deeply. It crept under my skin and began to infuse my being as a living experience and when, three years later, I was faced with having to let go of every thing I held dear in life, I found myself resting in an ocean of wholeness – a wholeness so complete that nothing outside of me could make it more so, nor could anything detract from it. The wholeness was simply, completely complete.

Often, we become attached to something or someone because deep down we fear we wouldn't be complete without them. We fear letting go into the presence of the unknown, and feel that we would be left bereft, lost, alone without that outer possession, person, lifestyle. Indeed, some of us have become so identified with these things that we experience them as our actual identity . . . I'm Mr or Mrs so-and-so . . . I'm a teacher, engineer, business person . . . I live in . . . My children are . . . My lifestyle is . . . I, I, I, . . . My, my, my, . . .

Sometimes this identity can become so real for us that without it we fear there would be nothing or no one there. We fear non-existence.

Even in the asking, 'Who would I be without my car, job, money, husband, wife, family, profile, material possessions, home, friends, contacts,' an internal scrambling for something to cling to arises. Because of this, it's no wonder that attachment to outer things comes up as a common experience for nearly all of us.

Then, when some spiritually arrogant youngster, posing as an all-knowing guru or enlightened sage, has the nerve to tell us that the key to Freedom lies in non-attachment, we feel indignant. 'He's a monk – what does he know about "true" attachment. I'm not really a materialist,' you hear yourself say. 'It's natural to be attached to your loved ones, committed to your job, invested in your lifestyle, proud of what you've achieved, cherishing of the hard won possessions you've acquired through years of dedicated work. Of course it's *normal* to feel attached to a home you put all your love and care into, to the knowledge you've spent years attaining. How could something as natural as valuing what you've made of yourself and your life keep you from true freedom?'

These are all sentiments I might have agreed with fifteen years ago – until I heard the following story. In the hearing of it, mysteriously and effortlessly, the strings of attachment began to loosen their grip and over time melt away naturally. I didn't even know it had happened until I was confronted by a real life experience of losing everything I loved.

You might like to get really comfy and open your heart, the way a small child does when it's getting ready to listen to a really intriguing bedtime story. Just open your being and relax.

Once upon a time, a long, long time ago, there was an enlightened master who was also a very wealthy family man and the owner of several factories. He and his devoted disciple were casually strolling through a remote and dusty village one day, when they came upon a shop displaying antiques, bric-a-brac and odds and ends. There, in the shop window, was a totally unexpected item that caused the master to pause for a closer look. It was a porcelain teacup, sitting all on its own, and when he peered more closely at it he realised it was the very same, rare, prized teacup he had been seeking for over thirty years. He owned the other eleven cups, and now he'd finally found the one remaining cup that would complete his priceless tea set, the rarest of its kind, passed down from the rajas of old.

He was thrilled at his great good fortune and felt that grace had smiled upon him on this propitious day, for thirty years is a long time to be searching for a cup.

Now the shopkeeper, standing in the shadows just out of sight, spied the enlightened master gazing at his window and his heart leapt up into his throat, 'My god! He's finally turned up! This is my lucky day. Everyone knows this master is a very wealthy man. After thirty years, my wife and I can finally retire. This is the one teacup he needs to complete the rarest set in the world . . . we've got it made!' he gleefully exulted, as he licked his lips and rubbed his hands together.

He told his wife to hide in the kitchen. The gods had smiled upon them, and they could finally close the shop and take their longed for pilgrimage to the holy city of Varanasi. They could live like kings, and would never want for anything again.

Eager to welcome the master, the shopkeeper opened the door, and with a low sweeping bow he welcomed him and his disciple into the shop. He donned his most ingratiating smile, and with a smarmy, oily voice said, 'Namasté, swamiji. How can I help you today?'

The master gently explained that he was interested in the teacup in the window. 'Ah, well,' replied the shopkeeper, 'that is my most precious piece. Perhaps you are aware that it's the rarest of its kind in the world. It belongs to a set of twelve, and it's the last one.'

'Yes,' said the master, 'I'm very familiar with the set. It's a favourite of mine. I'd like to purchase that cup. What is your asking price?'

The shopkeeper's mouth became dry and his heart began to pound. He thought, 'This swami knows the unique rarity of the cup. He'll pay whatever I say,' and in the excitement of the moment named an astronomical price.

Upon hearing the price, the master simply replied, 'I'm sorry, kind sir, but I will only pay *this* amount,' and named a generous and equitable price. 'It is a fair price.'

The shopkeeper was taken aback. He had thought it was going to be easier than this; after all, an enlightened master is not some fishmonger who haggles in the market. Disconcerted, but not too discouraged, the shopkeeper dropped his asking price by a half, explaining to the master what a loss it would be to him, reiterating that the cup was the only remaining one of its kind.

The master acknowledged that indeed it was true. The cup was irreplaceable – the rarest available and, simply stated, that he would only pay *this* price, the original price he had offered. 'It is a fair price.'

Completely befuddled, the shopkeeper began scrambling internally. 'OK. OK. So this master wants to bargain. I'll take it down by yet half again, that's it. I'll still end up a wealthy man,' he said to himself.

With an unconvincing smile, and no excuse ready to hand, he said, 'Swamiji, you really do drive a hard bargain. OK. Let me tell you what I'll do. I'll reduce it by half again, but that's it – it's my final offer.'

The master's face saddened a little, and in a quiet voice he simply replied, 'I'm sorry sir. I guess you didn't understand me. I will pay only *this* price. It's a fair price.'

He motioned to his devotee that the time had come to conclude their stay, namastéd to the shopkeeper, and quietly walked out the door.

When they were but fifty paces down the road, they heard someone calling, shouting, and when they turned to look, it was the shopkeeper running after them, flailing, out of breath, pleading with them, 'Swamiji, swamiji, come back, please come back . . . You can have the cup at your price.'

And so they returned and did the transaction quite amicably. The shopkeeper of course secretly knew that he and his wife were set for life. The master knew this too, and both were well pleased.

While the deal was being concluded and the teacup was being wrapped, the devotee noticed a magnificent sabre up on the wall, just above the shopkeeper's head. He could not take his eyes off this sword – it was the most intricately designed, yet powerfully strong looking sabre he had ever seen. When he turned to avert his eyes, he found his gaze was constantly drawn back to it. He felt mesmerised by the sword.

He thought, 'I must have it. I'll call it my "sword of truth". It will take the highest place of honour in my house, just above the altar. Never before have I seen such a handsome sword. I simply *must* have it.'

'I am a man of modest means,' he figured, 'but if I do exactly what the master did, maybe I can get it at a vastly reduced price.'

So, trying to sound very unassuming and a little disinterested, the disciple casually motioned to the sword up on the wall, and said to the shopkeeper, 'That's an attractive sword you've got up there. I haven't got much use for it, but I'd like to know the asking price.'

The shopkeeper looked the devotee penetratively in the eyes. He was a shrewd man and, though he lived a humble life, he did not like to be toyed with. Pretence left a bad taste in his mouth. Nonetheless, feeling pleasantly disposed as he'd already made the sale of a lifetime, he decided to be generous, and he named an only slightly inflated price.

The devotee feigned a gasp, and said, 'No kind sir, I will pay only *this* price. It's a fair price,' imitating the master to a tee.

The shopkeeper, always happy to barter, for that after all was how the game was played, dropped the price by half.

The devotee winced, and said, 'No sir. I will pay only *this* price. It's a fair price.' And the shopkeeper dropped the price again.

The devotee finally shrugged his shoulders and said, 'I guess you didn't understand, sir . . . I will only buy the sword at *this* price. It's a fair price.' And, as the master had now concluded his business, together the two quietly strolled out of the shop.

When they were fifty paces down the road, the devotee looked back to see if the shopkeeper had followed them, but no, the shop door remained closed. In silence he and the master continued walking, the devotee sneaking glances over his shoulder every so often, completely nonplussed that the shopkeeper had not come chasing after him. He'd done everything the master had done. Why hadn't it worked?

When they paused for a drink, a mile down the road, the disciple finally spoke up. 'Master, why hasn't the shopkeeper come running after me the way he came after you?' The master, a man of few words, remained silent.

'But why didn't he follow us?' the devotee insisted.

Finally, the master spoke. 'Do you still thirst for that sword?'

'Well, yes master,' the devotee replied, 'Of course I do.'

'That shopkeeper can *smell* your thirst. He knows you lust for that sabre, and he also knows that when he opens his shop tomorrow morning, you'll be his first customer, and you'll take it at *his* price.'

The disciple was silent for a moment, as he let the words sink in, then petulantly asked, 'But master, did you not thirst for that teacup? You searched for it for over thirty years. Didn't you crave to complete your set?'

The master was silent, and in the quiet, the student realised that of course the master had not lusted for a mere cup. A little ashamed that he had been so audacious to presume that a master would crave for anything, he humbly asked, 'But what is your secret, master?'

And the master quietly answered, 'He came after me because he knew that I genuinely meant it when I said I would take it at a fair price – I was unattached. With you he could *smell* your lust, and he knows you'll be back.'

'But how can you not crave a cup that completes your rarest of collections?'

'Let me tell you my secret,' replied the master, 'Every night, before I go to bed, I get down on my hands and knees, and I thank God with all my heart for all the blessings of the day. And then, with my whole being, I offer up to God everything I hold dear. I offer up my factories, my ashram, my homes. I offer up my students, my friends and even my beloved wife and precious children – in my mind's eye I see the factories and ashram burnt down, I see my family and loved ones taken from me and resting in God's arms. And when my prayer is finished, I go to sleep a poor man.

'When I wake up, I look around me to greet the fresh, new day, and I see God's grace is still surrounding me. And, flooded with gratitude, I get down on my knees and I thank God with all my heart that for one more day he has blessed me with these priceless gifts. I realise that I am only His caretaker. These gifts were never *mine* to begin with. They have only ever been on loan. *Everything is on loan.*'

* * *

Everything *is* on loan.

When I heard these words, they had a profound effect on me. They penetrated deeply, and when I arrived home after the retreat with Gurumayi, I made a silent vow that I would take this teaching into my life. Like the master in the story, each night I would take a few moments to sincerely thank God for all the blessings of the day, and would offer up to grace all that was dear to me – our home, our family, our lifestyle, my marriage, our possessions and all our material wealth. And I found that each morning I arose with a heart full of gratitude, overwhelmed that I had been blessed for yet one more day.

My relationships to the physical things around me began to take on a quality of lightness. I was fully aware that they really didn't belong to me. They were a gift from grace, and my responsibility or dharma lay in cherishing them, honouring them and savouring the blessedness of having them around me.

I also began to view my relationships with people differently. My relationship with my daughter felt extremely precious and I viewed it as a profound blessing, and I felt an even deeper honouring take place in my marriage.

Everything around me began to feel special. Everything seemed imbued with a light, scintillating quality. I became aware of the ephemeral nature of all things in life – how short a time we really have on this planet, and how lucky we are to have the bountiful blessings we are surrounded with.

It was a simple, innocent practice, but its teachings continued to reverberate with deeper and deeper lessons about the fleeting nature of existence and how it is our gift to cherish it while it lasts.

In caring for the things around me, I also found that part of the gift was to pass on to others the blessing that had been given so graciously to me. And I began to notice that the material things in my life were able to come and go gracefully, and the completeness and gratitude I was resting in remained untouched. After a while, it became clear there was no ownership abiding anywhere – just life dancing in a vaster context of grace.

A paradox unfolded in my life. There was the profound recognition that everything was on loan, and therefore a blessing to be cherished; yet there was also a totally non-personal acceptance of letting the cherished things pass gracefully out of my life and into others' hands if gace so desired. I loved the gift dearly, yet felt completely neutral and unattached in its leave-taking. It really became a rich but *light* relationship with the outer things in my life.

Three years after the retreat, I was working in New York City when I received a phone call from a close friend in California. Our modest house on the beach in Malibu, which had been our family home, and which held everything that was materially dear to me – photographs, writing, mementos of family holidays, anniversary presents, inherited porcelain, beloved books, journals, wedding pictures – eighteen years of accumulated memories, had burned down in a huge forest fire. We were financially devastated, and materially wiped out.

I remember so clearly hearing the news, and waiting to feel a big thud in my guts, because, of course, the truth of the matter was there would never be any way of replacing these priceless things. We'd lived a modest life to begin with, so worries of how we would get back on our feet and get a roof over our head were the fears I *expected* to feel, but they didn't manifest!

Instead I felt curiously light, as if some old karma had been lifted off my shoulders – as if a huge weight had fallen away. All of those things had only ever been on loan, and the gratitude and completion I was resting in felt *completely untouched.*

Those of you who have read my first book, *The Journey*, will know that the fire was just the beginning of a huge wave of leave-taking that happened over the course of the next two years.

A year later, my marriage unexpectedly dissolved, my daughter became estranged, and the tax authorities ended up taking all our finances. Everything I had come to know as my lifestyle fell away and I was left utterly and literally without anything.

And yet, this infinite grace that I was resting in felt so abundant, so full. I can honestly say with my hand on my heart, the wholeness did *not* become less whole. It just became more openly apparent! Of course, the natural experience of grieving, loss, hurt and letting go took place. But it happened in the vaster context of feeling already whole and completely complete.

Over the last several years, grace has blessed me with new relationships, a new deeply rewarding marriage, an entirely new business, bestselling books and a lifestyle so charmed and full of grace that even in my dreams I could not have imagined it.

And yet, I am still aware that *everything in my life is still and always was on loan*. I dance an even lighter relationship with the outer things in my life. The gratitude deepens; the recognition that life is truly fleeting and each precious drop of it must be savoured has become even sharper, and the extraordinary blessedness has only become more poignant.

Truly, non-attachment is your invitation to soar in complete freedom.

✲ ✲ ✲

Attachment to *outer* things is not the only attachment we have in our lives. There is a subtler, equally powerful but more insidious attachment that happens in our *inner* lives – attachment to our thoughts, our acquired knowledge and learned beliefs.

Many of us have trained in certain fields, have become schooled, learned and expert in various professions, disciplines and aspects of life. In addition, our life experience has given rise to beliefs that we have come to hold as truth. We have subtly become attached to these beliefs. They may serve as a pseudo-refuge in the known, becoming conceptual security blankets that can seem to evolve into concrete reality. When we have the certain belief that this view of the world is the way things really are, we give tacit permission to ourselves to stop investigating life. There's no longer a need to view life freshly because we have our beliefs to fall back on, and our curiosity gets stifled and our natural awe and wonder becomes unavailable.

The 'known' then becomes a dead thing, born entirely from our past references, and we carry it around like so much baggage – dragging our beliefs and our certainties along with us, never bothering to truly question their current validity or usability in our lives.

With the knowledge of how things are, we no longer need to open freshly in life. Instead, we hide behind our knowledge, smug that we know better than others, losing sight of our innocence and receptivity to all things.

With so much dead wood floating around in our minds, it doesn't even occur to us to question the truth of our apparent reality. Then our beliefs become the very prison that keeps us from experiencing freedom, grace and truth in the present moment.

Indeed, our attachment to this lifeless, outdated, acquired knowledge can prevent us from fully experiencing life. We end up seeing everything through the filters of our beliefs, and while life carries on joyously, miraculously, creating itself anew in each moment, we remain stuck in the old – just because we won't give up our well-backed-up beliefs.

Finally, it is when we cast off everything we *think* is true, all that we *know*, that freedom finally becomes available in the *un*known. It's when we let go of all our knowing that infinite wisdom can reveal itself.

There is a beautiful story that has been passed down from teacher to student for hundreds of years. It's an invitation to drop all the dead wood of what we hold to be true, and to finally open into the freshness of the unknown.

So, let your awareness grow spacious and become curious like a child, as you let this inspiring parable do its work.

Once upon a time, there was a great seeker of truth, who longed with all his heart to directly experience enlightenment – to have and to embody the wisdom of the liberated masters.

Believing that the masters attained their enlightenment from spiritual texts, this seeker set out on a path to know and imbibe every great spiritual text known to man. He learned the Upanishads, mastered the 27,000 verses of the Ramayana, could recite the Vedas, and learned all the spiritual knowledge behind the Vedic rituals; he dived into the Mahabharata, memorising each syllable. He knew the St James version of the Bible, and devoured rare, ancient translations not found in the local libraries. He mastered all the mantras, and the many forms of yoga were all second nature to him. He could recite huge tracts of the Koran and studied the Torah deeply and fully. There was no spiritual book he had not read, no technique he had not learned, no ritual left unexperienced and no mantra left to learn.

By now he was sixty years old, and was considered the greatest spiritual scholar of his time. No one could better him in a debate, for he would undoubtedly know some obscure fact from some rare text to overturn any academic argument. So identified with all his accolades, spiritual merit and knowledge had he become, that he was thought of as intellectually invincible.

But in his heart of hearts he sensed, he *knew*, that somehow he still wasn't complete. Enlightenment had eluded him, and as there was no more knowledge that could be attained, he decided it was time to seek out an enlightened master.

He had heard there was an old sage hermited on the top of a mountain in the Himalayas and, though it would be a long and arduous journey, he fervently hoped he'd get the final knowledge he needed to be enlightened. So, carrying only his rarest, most precious books and the supplies he needed, he began his trek.

After three weeks and three days, he was only two-thirds of the way there. His baggage had become heavy, and he was growing weary. How could he lighten his load? Item by item, he turned over his possessions, 'Oh, I couldn't give up *that* book – it's the only one of its kind in the world. Oh, and *that* text was given to me as an award for outstanding scholarly merit – I couldn't possibly give up that one.' He found that he could throw none of them away. To him, they represented the sum total of all his knowledge. They were priceless and irreplaceable; they were an integral part of him.

Instead, he began to throw away what other supplies he could afford to lose. This tin cup – he could drink water from a stream in his cupped hands, after all. This heavy plate – he could use a palm leaf as a dish. And he only needed one knife – all other silverware could be discarded. And so, in this way he lightened his load and continued his strenuous journey up the mountain.

Nine days later he finally arrived at the master's hermitage, perched at the very edge of a cliff. Exhausted and weary he told the master's attendant that he had travelled a huge distance just to receive the final teaching of enlightenment. 'Please tell the master I am a learned man, a scholar who has mastered all the spiritual texts, the mantras and all the Vedas. I do not want to waste his time. I do not need to learn any more texts. I want only to receive the knowledge of enlightenment.'

The attendant nodded his head, went to the master's hut, delivered the message, then returned to the expectant seeker. 'The master says he has heard your message, and he will call you when he is ready!'

'But I am a busy and important man. I did not come all this way to be put through some rudimentary teaching. There is nothing more for me to learn. I know every text off by heart. I'm only here to secure enlightenment. I haven't got a lot of time to waste.'

The attendant took the message into the master's hut, and returned with the master's reply. 'He will see you when he is ready. He is engaged right now.'

Three days passed in just this way: the academic asking for permission to see the master, and the master too busy to see him. Then, when the attendant came back one more time to deliver the same message, the academic finally, in exasperation, pushed him aside, strode over to the hut, threw open the door and stepped straight into the master's room – a simple room, with just a mat and two cushions on the floor.

The enlightened sage was sitting on one cushion boiling some water to make tea. He looked up at the man and said nothing as he went back to making his tea.

Dumbfounded, the venerated scholar, who was used to being treated with the highest respect, could only plonk himself down on the cushion and wait for the master to speak. But the master said nothing. He seemed more interested in the tea-leaves in his cup than in the man who had just arrived in his hut.

Exasperated and infuriated, the famous academician finally spoke out. He began by counting out all of his doctoral degrees, listing the countless spiritual tomes he had mastered, explaining that he knew all the rituals, was a master at yoga and was considered the most spiritually knowledgeable man in all the land. He explained that he had only come to the master to receive the knowledge of enlightenment and, as he was a busy and important man, did not want to waste either his own or the master's time with anything unnecessary. He already knew all there was to know, and had only come so he could get the final teaching.

The master listened as he spoke, and when he was finished, turned his attention back to the tea. When the brew was perfect, the master finally spoke, 'Will you join me for some tea?'

Angry that the master did not seem to understand the urgency or importance of his request, the scholar shrugged his shoulders, agreed to tea and proceeded to reiterate all he had said before, but this time louder and more pointedly, as he punctuated the more impressive bits and put greater emphasis on the particular learning he felt would cause the master to respond.

When he was done, again the master remained silent and simply began pouring the tea into a cup. The cup became full and then began to overflow, the tea spilling all over the dirt floor.

Jumping up, so as not to get burned by the tea, the scholar shouted, 'Master, master! Stop pouring! The cup is overflowing! Can't you see?' – thinking to himself that the sage must have gone batty in his old age.

The master finally looked up at the scholar, and said simply, 'Yes, I see perfectly . . . You are like this cup – so full of all your ideas, concepts, knowledge and learned wisdom that I have nothing to give you. The grace of true knowledge cannot flow into a cup that is already full – it would only pour over the sides and go wasted. If you truly want what you say you came here to receive, take all your precious books and make some *good* use of them: use them for fuel, burn them, for it is cold here. Then take all your awards and certificates and give them to the children of the village to play with, for they are nought but trinkets, toys for the delight of infants. And then, once your cup is truly empty, we can share some tea together. Then perhaps you'll receive what you came here to experience.'

* * *

Freedom can only be experienced in the emptiness of non-attachment: non-attachment to our ideas, beliefs and acquired knowledge, all of which are merely mental constructs born from the dead wood of our past, and which take our attention away from what is always here – the freshness of the present moment. These constructs act as filters that colour and distort reality. When you choose to let go of all you *think* you know, all the filters drop away, and unobscured awareness is all that remains. All enlightenment is realised to be here. It is in subtracting the known that the infinite presence of the *un*known is realised.

Your learned expertise, acquired notions and accumulated beliefs are like mud on your windscreen of reality – when you take Windex and wash it clean, you are left as crystal clear consciousness, sparkling presence.

It is said that those who *know*, don't know, and those who *don't know*, know.

Resting in all innocence in the willingness to not know *anything*, truth is revealed. *Anything* you are attached to – be it the internal world of mental constructs, beliefs or expertise; or the external world of relationships, lifestyle or material possessions – if you collapse all of your awareness into it, will cause you to lose sight of the large context in which everything appears.

And yet, you can remain wide open and allow all of the play of manifestation to dance lightly through your open awareness. You can delight in it, take great joy from it, and always remain aware of the vaster context in which it is all appearing. In this way you are neither invested in your outer material world, nor collapsed into your inner mental constructs. All is free to come effortlessly through consciousness – no clinging, no grasping, no reaching, no identification, *no attachment.*

Just *this.* Open freedom, enlightened presence.

Guided Introspection – Non-Attachment

Again, there are a number of ways you can do this process. Either use your companion CD, record yourself reading the passage below or ask a friend, from an open, spacious place to read it to you. Or, once again you could just start by taking in a few slow, deep breaths, keeping your awareness soft and spacious, and read it as an open-eyed meditation, allowing the words to carry you deep within.

Allow yourself to find a quiet place, where you feel comfortable and at ease, and let your being settle. Feel your awareness becoming spacious, and open.

In this guided introspection, it is important to take plenty of time to pause and allow your own internal response to arise naturally, in its own time, from the depths of your being. In this particular form of self-inquiry, you might receive a word-less response – more of a simple inner knowing, or you might experience a feeling of expansion or vastness.

Let it all just happen naturally. It really is a process of self-discovery.

Enlightened presence is naturally experienced when the bonds of attachment have loosened, dissolved and been set free. Any grasping, holding, reaching for the known – be it in the form of ideas, beliefs, learned knowledge – contracts your being. Any holding onto or identifying with belongings, relationships, material possessions, lifestyles only keeps us feeling separate from the infinite.

The willingness to experience what remains after all of the 'known' has dropped away is a key to freedom.

You can begin by allowing your awareness to become spacious in front. . . feeling it become vast and open behind . . . infinite to all sides . . . boundless below . . . and vast above . . . vast inside . . . vast outside . . . vastness everywhere.

So, resting in all spaciousness, you can start asking yourself these questions. If you're reading this to yourself, once you've listened to a question, close your eyes and feel yourself opening to receive a response from within. At first, words might arise, but as you continue to inquire, you might feel yourself falling into a vast, boundless presence of grace where words and thoughts are absent. Be willing to experience it however *you* experience it.

1. If all the outer things you've identified with in the past, your material goods, your family, your lifestyle were taken away, what would remain? . . . Who would remain? . . . who are you really without all these things? . . . Who are you?

2. If you did not have all your beliefs, constructs, ideas,

learned knowledge, expertise; if all that fell away, what would remain? . . . Who are you?

3. If you could not define yourself in terms of anything – no role or job, no acquired knowledge, no car, home, relationship. If all these were not there, who would you be? . . . what would remain? . . . Who are you?

4. Without all the labels and road signs that point to you, identifying you, defining you, would there be anyone there? . . . Without all the trappings, who would you be? . . . Who are you?

5. If you could not use your family, background, your possessions, your knowledge, your material wealth or your job in order to relate to, or connect with others, what would be left? . . . Who would you be? . . . Who would be the speaker? . . . What would be speaking through you? . . . Who are you?

6. If all labels dropped away, and you sincerely opened and asked: 'Who am I?' what would arise? . . .
   Who are you? . . .
   Who are you *really*? . . .
   What remains? . . .
   Who are you?

Just rest now in the unobscured presence of your own essence, and then when you're ready you may gently open your eyes.

All of manifestation is welcome to dance lightly through the vast, open expanse of your own being.

present-moment awareness

There is a real power in bringing
your awareness into the now.

When all of your being is surrendered
to just this moment, fully present,
freedom is revealed to already be here.

There is a great power in the simplicity of bringing all of your focus, attention, awareness to the present moment. Indeed, when all thought has fallen away and all attention has become riveted in the present, the presence of grace, of truth, is automatically, instantaneously revealed to be already here.

It is a great mystery as to why this is so, but it is true nonetheless. In fact, when we explore the principle by checking out our own direct experience it becomes so apparent, so evident, that it's astonishing that we ever overlooked this simple, profound truth. When you bring your awareness to the moment, freedom is realised to be already here.

Why not try an experiment? Right now just bring all of your awareness to just this tiny moment . . . no thought of past . . . no thought of future . . . just *this* moment . . . Let your attention rest effortlessly on the words you are reading . . . Notice what the letters look like . . . Feel the weight of this book . . . Now feel the thickness of the page you are reading . . . You might even notice the faint scent of the paper . . . or the smells in the room . . . Let your being settle . . . Know that for this tiny instant all awareness can gently come to rest in just *this moment*. Perhaps there are sounds in the background . . . Let yourself relax in the awareness of them . . . Take your time . . . *Just be present to this moment.*

If you find your mind is straining, or efforting to focus, soften the tension or contraction in your brain. As a matter of fact, let your awareness become aware of any opening or closure going on in the mind. If you let your awareness remain vast and open without any desire to change anything, the contraction or tension of mind will relax and open naturally . . . Just staying wide open, notice how the mind feels as it relaxes and opens . . . Now become aware of what the mind is appearing *in* . . . Become aware of awareness itself . . . What is body appearing in? . . . What are thoughts appearing in? . . . What are emotions arising in? . . . Be still and present to *just this moment.*

What is here?

If you are really just *being* here now, in this moment, with no thought other than awareness being riveted to this instant, you will become aware of a stillness inherent here . . . a vastness . . . a spaciousness. It's always here. Freedom always is. Yet for so long we have put our awareness everywhere *but here*. Presence can only be experienced when all awareness is riveted in this moment.

For centuries yogis, recognising the power of a still mind riveted in the present moment, have tried to harness the attention of the mind by *forcing* it to focus on the divine, by riveting it onto a specific object, or focusing it on a deity. They have written volumes on how to train the mind to become still by attending to specific sounds or repeating certain mantras or prayers. They have taught their students how to focus on candle flames, asanas, chakras, inner lights, trying to still the constant motion of the so called 'monkey mind'. They literally try to use the mind to still the mind, all the while believing that if only we can get the mind to stop we'll experience the infinite stillness, mind-free awareness.

And though it is true that when mind talk slows down and falls away, open, free awareness is revealed to be already present; it is equally true that this very forcing, training, efforting, willing, cajoling, judging of thought can push the experience of freedom further and further away, so stillness continues to elude us. One cannot use mind talk to stop mind talk, for as soon as the will relaxes all thoughts naturally come flooding back into consciousness. It's like trying to use a dirty cloth to clean up a mess. You just get a bigger mess.

What if there was nothing wrong with the mind? What if the real mistake lay in *resisting and judging* our thoughts? What if the real problem was in wishing the thoughts weren't there and trying to will them away; or worse, battling with them, trying to overcome them with willpower, sounds, mantras or vacuous positive affirmations.

What if our thoughts had no meaning whatsoever, except the meaning we choose to give them? And what if we realised that thoughts are really just a bunch of syllables trailing though consciousness? Can you get a sense of how giving all this energy, attention, will, struggle and import to thought only perpetuates the very thing you wish to be free from? It's a futile, counterproductive venture.

What if your own experience was of being an open sky of awareness, effortlessly resting in the moment, giving your full attention to whatever is here in front of you now? And what if thoughts were allowed to waft through awareness *without* you engaging in or attending to them? What would that be like?

For me, I feel a keen alertness, a spaciousness, a present moment-ness and thoughts waft through the open sky of awareness like a flock of birds. I can hear their distant call but the open sky is untouched by the noise or the movement. My attention is effortlessly riveted in this moment – effortlessly in the now, and the birds are none of my business. Awareness is simply aware that they've flown through.

It feels relaxing, true, open. And it is totally effortless. Any efforting is an invitation to *stop*, open and be present.

But the truth is most of us *like* to be entertained by our thoughts. We find them fascinating. Maybe we believe our own story of past pain, injustice, hurt. We believe our victim-ness defines us. Who would we be without all the stories of the past to examine and re-examine, add to and perpetuate? We believe they give us meaning and context.

But what if that were all just a lie? What if our past was just that – *past, gone*? The reality is it's *not* here right now. In order to bring the pain, torment and hurt forward, you have to *choose* to welcome them into your present awareness, then you have to feed the flame of that pain, add fuel to the fire, using your thoughts to enhance and heighten a pain that is not even here as part of the present moment.

Only this moment is here and, thank goodness, life loves you enough to give you the choice each moment: Do I follow my thoughts, lay a nice feast for them, give them my energy, my attention, add colour, flavour, spice to them, make them all important; or do I stay as open sky, notice thoughts coming though awareness, pay them no heed, feeling that they truly are none of my business, and allow them to come and allow them to go?

Open sky is *not* touched by what comes through it.

However, if we pluck the birds out of the sky – feed them, admire them, imbue them with our love, trap them, hold them and decide that they give our life meaning, and worse still, when they fly away (as they inevitably will, because thoughts are only fleeting experiences that last only as long as you hold them in your consciousness) give ourselves permission to use them as a weapon to blame others, or life, for the pain we're in – we can fuel our story of suffering in perpetuity. We can even make a lifestyle out of our story, calling our friends to gossip about our thoughts and enlisting their support in blaming others for them. Or we can go to therapists to analyse them, pull them apart, until we are consumed by 'me and my story of pain'. Then the worship of thought becomes our religion, our identity, our life.

Or, you can just *stop the game*.

I have a definition of free will that is based in science. In recent years scientists have found that *before* any thought gives rise to itself there is a momentary pause, a tiny synapse, which occurs just before the thought comes up. In that split second you are given the choice: Do I follow the thought, give it all my attention, intensify my story of pain and use it to blame others, or life, or myself; or do I *stop*, stay open – aware of the open sky of awareness – and allow thought to give rise to itself and flow unattended through open consciousness, like so many distant birds soaring through the sky?

The choice is yours, and is available to you each and every moment. You are free to follow your thoughts, creating self-induced pain, and you are free to allow thoughts to effortlessly come and go, letting them be none of your business. It's up to you to choose or not.

Over the years I have become so bored with my thoughts, so tired of my story, that nowadays when thoughts come it feels like too much effort to even bother to listen to them, to take notice of them, or even believe in them. I just don't believe in the story my mind creates anymore. I know mind talk is just a string of syllables coming through consciousness, and it has *no* significance other than the significance I choose to attribute to it.

The fascinating and wondrous thing is that, because I am so disinterested in thoughts of the past, and even less interested in constructing painful imagery of the future, my thoughts have become bored with *me*. They realise I am not going to feed them, be seduced by them or give them any energy, and so they often don't bother showing up at all. They realise they're not going to get my attention, because I genuinely don't believe they have any meaning. So, long periods of time are spent in thought-free awareness. Not because I willed it, or concentrated on mantras, or repeated affirmations, or forced or trained my mind, but just because I offer thoughts no resistance. I just can't imagine what entertainment value being made miserable by my self-chosen thoughts might have. So, innocently, I just rest in thought-free consciousness, and because my thoughts are bored with me and I'm bored with them, they don't bother arising.

Thoughts are free to come, thoughts are free to go. You can just rest in the open sky of awareness itself. It's so effortless, so freeing and so easy.

Why not try an experiment right now? (If you'd like you can turn on the companion CD and listen to my voice, or record your own voice giving this guided meditation.)

Close your eyes and gently become aware of awareness . . . Firstly allow yourself to become aware of how open and vast the awareness already is in front of you . . . how spacious and free it is behind . . . how vast and open it is to all sides . . . It's just free . . . Now, staying as this, put an 'all call' out to *all thoughts* – really put out a huge welcome – welcome all thoughts to come flooding into the vast open sky of your awareness . . . You can let it become a veritable din if need be, but just allow them all to come . . . You can even welcome not just your thoughts but all the thoughts that have ever existed . . . even all of humanity's thoughts.

Stay wide open and relax your body as you allow whatever thoughts want to come, to come pouring through consciousness . . . Stay still and open . . . Does any thought really touch the essential you? . . . Does it in any way affect open sky?

For many people, when they try this for the first time, they find themselves so at ease, so welcoming, so vast and so open that *no thoughts* even bother showing up.

This is a secret, a mystery. When no resistance is offered to thought, when all thoughts are fully welcomed, thoughts realise they are finally free to come or *not* come – they realise you are *not* going to resist them or engage in a battle with them and, usually, they feel so welcomed that they just rest undisturbed and the awareness remains open and free.

Sometimes, the first time you try this experiment a whole host of thoughts come flooding. If that is the case just admit the truth of your experience. Do these thoughts in any way touch, affect or alter freedom? Or does freedom, does spacious awareness, remain untouched by anything that comes through it? If you are open and honest in the experiment, you will notice that the essential you, presence, is absolutely untouched by *anything* that comes through it. So then the question again becomes: Do I choose to pull thoughts out of the sky, invest them with my energy, time, life force, letting my self-created, self-induced pain and drama be enhanced; or, do I allow thoughts to come and allow thoughts to go and just stay as open sky, in freedom?

The choice is yours and it's always available. It's the true definition of free will.

✲ ✲ ✲

Often we pay heed to our thoughts not to add drama to our life, but because finding answers is just plain fascinating. But the truth is the thinking mind can only give rise to answers we already know or have learned. It can only give conditioned responses. For the thinking mind is a trained animal and follows the rote, learned formulas we teach it.

On the other hand *infinite* mind is an unborn potential capable of giving rise to true genius, inspiration and free thought. But we are so in the habit of worshipping the learned and acquired mind-talk born from our thinking mind that our awareness is collapsed into the known. We have pat answers for everything. We 'knee-jerk react' our way through life. For true inspiration to arise we must open and *stay* open *freshly* in the *un*-known. There has to be a willingness *not* to know, not to have the answers ready-made for regurgitation upon command, not to resort to or fall back on known formulas, idioms or set cultural beliefs. There must be a willingness in *each moment* to rest easily in innocence, to be fully present to *this moment,* which can never be known in advance. There must be fresh openness to what life is revealing in each moment.

This entire book has been written from this open presence. I have not known in advance what was going to write itself onto a page. Even in the writing of that last sentence I did not know what would fall onto the page until *after* it was written down.

It takes courage to be willing *not* to know. And mainly it's a choice, a decision. To be totally open to this moment means *not* to consult your past ideas about what it might mean, nor to look to the future for what it could mean, but to be just here now, in what is here in this instant. Then the next moment will come and we are present to it. And the moment after that arrives and we are freshly open to it. Life then becomes a never-ending stream of moment-to-moment *nowness*. Always here, always now.

My dear friend Catherine Ingram, satsang teacher and author of the book *Passionate Presence*, often shares a wonderful metaphor that I find useful in staying present to the moment.

A favourite question of the thinking mind is to ask, 'Why?' Of course that will only lead us into an endless morass of seeking and confusion, questioning and wondering. And it takes us directly out of what is being revealed right here, right now. If the 'Why' question arises, like, 'Why is the sky blue?' 'Why did a picture of my mum just come through awareness?' 'Why is that person doing that?' 'Why can't I get it right?' . . . (ad nauseum!) it takes us directly into mind and out of the moment.

Catherine likes to suggest that we use an imaginary bucket. She calls it the bucket of unknowables. I sometimes refer to it as a mystery bucket, and we throw all questions of 'Why' into it. 'Why is the sky blue?' – Don't know, in the bucket. 'Why did my mum's picture just come through consciousness?' – Don't know, in the bucket. 'Why can't I get it right?' – Don't know, in the bucket.

It's so simple, yet so powerful. Honestly, these days it feels like my whole life is in the bucket!

Why not try it for yourself right now? Releasing 'Why' questions into the unknown allows you to keep all your awareness right here, right now. Simply ask a 'Why' question, maybe a question you've been struggling with life. Now feel what it feels like to give the immediate reply 'Don't know,' and then imagine tossing the whole question into the bucket of unknowables. Can you feel how easy and freeing it is?

Some of you might be saying, 'Yes, but how am I going to *know* what to *do* in any given moment?' My experience is that the *infinite* intelligence knows *exactly* what to do each and every moment, and not only that, but it has an uncannily divine appropriateness to its knowing. It knows how and when to brush your teeth, add up the numbers on your tax form, care for your child, file your papers at work. When you bring your full attention to *whatever* you are doing, be it washing the dishes, listening to a friend, or going through digital information, in the stillness grace will find the appropriate response, answer or action. But endlessly asking, 'Why this?' 'Why that?' only takes us out of the moment, and we become less efficient, less elegant, less graceful and sometimes totally ineffectual.

I was recently talking to Tricia, one of our European Journey staff members, and she was telling me how powerful a killer of action taking her awareness away from the present is. She said that when there is lots to do, if she let her awareness be drawn to catastrophic pictures of the future, where she'd be overwhelmed by work and unable to cope with it; or if she let her awareness drift back to the past, referencing times she'd just not got it right, she would become so overcome with the impossibility of it all – feeling the guilt from the past and incapacitating fear of the future – her awareness would collapse completely and her body would go into shut-down mode. Then nothing would get done – nothing whatsoever.

Then she shared her tried and tested strategy for freedom. She said that the moment she recognises this old pattern she sees through the game and chooses to just stop, bring her awareness right to the moment and give all of her love and attention to the task in front of her. Effortlessly and instantly she becomes present. In being present she finds ease, grace, freedom and absolutely *no* stress whatsoever – and activity takes place efficiently, effortlessly.

Stress is born from our willingness to take up residence in debilitating pictures of the past, or from collapsing our awareness into imaginary limiting pictures of the future.

The good news is you have a choice. You can decide to reside in the stress or step into the magic, beauty and elegant efficiency that is here when all awareness is riveted to the *now*.

Freedom is a choice.

So, if a 'Why' is arising, just *stop*. Say, 'Don't know,' and throw the question into your bucket of unknowables. Simply bring your awareness back to the task in front of you. The freedom and release you feel will astound you.

✲ ✲ ✲

I recently had a potent and beautiful reminder of the magic of what grace can accomplish when your being is riveted and surrendered into the timelessness of the present moment. Even in the most pressured, stressed and hectic circumstances, if you are willing to give all of yourself to the moment, miracles can happen.

Over the past few years it seems that my seminar schedule has become increasingly booked. With so many countries on different continents thirsting for the work, I found I was teaching forty-four out of fifty-two weeks in a year, with writing, media, press and family holidays slotting into the few remaining weeks left. And it's not just been how much time has been devoted to offering the work, but also how much travelling is required within that schedule, as I am always on a global tour, travelling all over Europe, the UK, on to America then Australia and New Zealand, back through South Africa, to return to the UK only to start the more advanced seminars and retreats and begin the world tour again.

To say the tour takes place at a breathless yet constant pace is an understatement. Often, when people say to me, 'My god Brandon, you have three times more seminars and retreats than any teacher out there; how do you do it?' I can only shrug and honestly admit that it must be grace; for surely if I had to do all the doing, the weight of such a relentless schedule would be impossible to bear. But as I can only be in one place at one time and only be present to the task at hand, in the present moment, there is nowhere else to go.

I can only be in this moment, right now. I find I can't afford to drag the previous moment into this one, and I don't have the time or energy to be contemplating what could, should or might take place in the future, for it would only scare me to see the magnitude of it all.

So, my job *requires* me to stay present to what's happening here, right now, in this moment. Any deviance from the now would only spin me into a huge energy drain.

This was never more evident than just three days ago, when I had agreed to be the celebrant creating an embrace for a wedding ceremony for two young employees, Maarten and Yvonne, here at my private home.

I had arrived home from my summer holidays and hit the ground running, with back-to-back meetings, a presenters' seminar, staff meetings, satsang and vision-questing, and was fully aware that I was going directly from the whirlwind of 'preparation week' into a full seminar tour with workshops and retreats all over Europe, South Africa and Australia.

If I'd allowed my mind, even for one moment, to fall into the trap of pondering all the upcoming events, I honestly feel I would have collapsed under the sheer weight of responsibility of all that lay ahead of me. But there was no time to dwell on what is not yet here, nor on what just took place. The reality is, there *is* only this moment, right now.

Maarten and Yvonne's wedding was going to take place in the midst of this whirlwind week, and still the occasion required a real honouring and reverence. It couldn't just be squeezed into a space between the other equally demanding events and put on the back burner.

The reason I share the whole background is because we often have the belief, 'If only I didn't have such a hectic schedule, if only everything were under control and in its place, I could take *time out to be present.*' This is a false notion that puts you on a path of postponement, and is completely untrue. Because, if you are fully present, even in the face of a whirlwind, grace manages appropriately and effortlessly to take care of all aspects of manifestation – if you are willing to surrender to attending only the needs of the moment. When our minds dangle wastefully on thoughts of the past or dwell in pictures of the future, our awareness is not focused and present to what is here right now. The task at hand takes twice as long because the mind is wandering elsewhere.

During the week of meetings and workshops leading up to this wedding, each time the bride and groom came over to consult with me about food, music, rental of equipment, timings, programmes, ushers, vows, readings, shopping, dress code, flowers, decoration, the outside pavilion, seating – well you know how it is, the list goes on and on – their meetings had to be sandwiched in between other business commitments, all of which were necessary, important and impossible to change. Yet in each meeting there was a timelessness as we effortlessly addressed the needs of the moment, taking time to offer our love and energy, opening our beings to allow grace to give rise to the inspiration needed to create a graceful, elegant wedding ceremony. Circumstances required me to stay completely riveted, patient and present to the myriad needs of the bridal couple.

As the wedding day came closer more action needed to take place: food to be purchased; plates, glasses, tablecloths to be hired; flower arrangements to be agreed; printed programmes to be made; music to be organised, and so on. This was not something that could be fobbed off on someone else. Each of these areas had to be addressed, honoured and actioned appropriately.

On Saturday, the day before the ceremony, as grace would have it a number of the Journey team and staff offered to pitch in to help, and they too effortlessly fell into action. As host, wedding organiser, caterer, decorator and officiant for the sacred celebration happening on Sunday, you might imagine that at some time I might have given myself permission, at least temporarily, to collapse in exhaustion under the pressure. But time did not allow for such indulgences. Complete surrender was the only option. And a remarkable, almost magical, phenomenon began to occur throughout the day. Outwardly, to all those who had entered the house at this time, it probably looked like a maelstrom of chaos, a hurricane of activity: I actually overheard someone who delivered something say, 'It's like a circus in here.' But somehow everyone was surrendered, lightly carrying on, going about the tasks of cooking, cleaning, decorating, arranging and miraculously turning our home into an exquisite chapel, a sacred, glorious sanctuary for the wedding.

In the midst of this hurricane, time felt as if it was beginning to stand still as I sat quietly, patiently with the wedding couple and meticulously and lovingly went through every final detail of the wedding day. I felt so open that it was as if everything and everyone around me was welcome in the embrace of that openness. *There was no resistance anywhere*. Frequently we were interrupted as my attention was drawn to oversee the flower arrangements or make some decision. I was asked for clear answers on everything from the placement of the pavilion, to arrangement of chairs and cushions, to where guests should park their cars. Someone asked if the bruschetta needed more spice. Someone else enquired how to operate the sound system.

Yet, curiously, amazingly, there seemed to be so much time. It actually felt like time expanded – that it was leisurely and gracious and there was plenty of time to answer all questions and take all decisions while remaining open, patient and honouring of the wedding couple. It felt so spacious that there was even room for new inspiration for the ceremony to spontaneously give birth to itself. And it's no surprise that the following day the wedding turned out to be glorious, sublime, absolutely infused with grace. All because total surrender to the moment allowed grace to flourish.

Recently I've begun to wonder if, when we surrender all of our being, consciousness, love, to the moment, perhaps time becomes illusory and grace takes over and begins doing the doing. Of course I can't know if this is true, but it is what it feels like.

Sometimes I say that nature abhors a void, and when you offer all of yourself to the needs of the moment – all of your thoughts, emotions, your being – when you surrender everything, it is as if an emptiness, a void, is left behind, and grace rushes in to fill the gap and does all the doing through you, as you. All I know is that it feels effortless – like being made of air, lightly dancing in freedom.

And it feels like no one is doing the doing. Somehow, life is dancing itself.

So, the invitation is to just *stop*. *Stop* giving excuses as to why you cannot be present. *Stop* entertaining thoughts of past or future. *Stop* asking why or how. *Stop* resisting the endless motion and activity of life. *Stop* your internal dialogue of, 'But, there's so much to do.' *Stop* resisting the way things are.

Simply stop.

The bliss of freedom is waiting for you, and it's revealed to be here the moment you give *all* of yourself to the *now*. The time has come to stop and open your whole being to life. The choice is yours. The discovery awaits you.

Freedom already is.

✡ ✡ ✡

Guided Introspection – Present-Moment Awareness

Finally, I wanted to offer you a process that I find particularly useful when there is a strong pattern of self-judgement going on internally. Self-judgement distracts us from the moment and keeps present-moment awareness at bay, taking us out of the now. It can act as a shroud, veiling the beauty of just this moment.

When judgement is understood, released, forgiven and let go, then all of your being is free to settle simply and easily into just this moment. Being here in the moment becomes easy, obvious and the beauty and grace inherent in the now is effortlessly exposed.

What follows is a very powerful process for releasing that judgement and it's one I introduce at seminars when a large portion of the audience seems stuck in self-blame, trapped in self-judgement, constantly listening to an inner critic that just won't shut up.

If your mind-talk is railroaded along lines of continual self-criticism it can grow very tiresome indeed, and I find the best way to handle it is to bring it out into the open, acknowledge the game and finally forgive yourself for being such a harsh judge. For the truth is that most of us are secretly very hard on ourselves, and this process can help penetrate the lie of the game and soften the ego's mind trip.

So, if you have it, you can turn on the companion CD now, or you can record yourself speaking the words and play them back to yourself, or get a friend to read them to you, so that you can listen to this guided process comfortably with your eyes closed.

Begin by closing your eyes and taking a few nice deep breaths in and sighing them out, letting your breath become slow and even. Then once again become aware of your awareness . . . Experience how spacious it already is in front . . . how vast it is behind . . . and feel the expansion to all sides . . . and just rest in a bath of stillness.

Now, in your mind's eye imagine a campfire. The nature of this campfire is unconditional love, all acceptance.

At this campfire there are only two people. There is a younger you, who can be any age from zero right up to now – so a flexible age range younger you.

And then of course there is the present-day you who has previously been full of judgements, blame and self-criticism.

If you look deeply at the younger you, you will see that the younger you feels so diminished, wretched in fact, for it seems no matter what the younger you did it was never good enough. And even when something did come out OK, there you were ready to point out how it could have been better.

The younger you has been made to fit the mould, to measure up to everyone else's harsh standards, and yet it seemed no matter how hard the younger you tried they just didn't measure up. They just weren't good enough.

And in all this blame and judgement, and in the face of all the internal criticism, the younger you lost sight of who they really are. They forgot the beauty, the magnificence, the grace of their true self, and instead tried to fit into everyone else's idea of how they should be. And still it was never enough.

If you look, or sense, or just know, you'll see the younger you feels wretched and in despair. So you might like to begin this campfire conversation by saying out loud to the younger you – (repeat out loud):

'I am so sorry for all the judgement . . . I've been so hard on you, no matter what you did, no matter how hard you tried, it was just never good enough for my impossibly harsh standards . . . I tried to make you fit the mould and when you couldn't get it exactly right, then I judged you some more . . . I've been so hard on you.

'I'm so sorry . . . I forgot that inside you is a real beauty, a real grace . . . Instead I bought into everyone else's ideas and concepts of how you should be and I lost sight of the *real* you . . . I'm so sorry . . . Please will you forgive me?'

Now open your own chest, as if opening a suit of armour, and allow all the forgiveness from the younger you to penetrate into the body and being of the present day you . . . taking your time and really opening to receive the forgiveness for all your judgement.

Then turn to the younger you and say, 'I'm so sorry I lost sight of the real you, and tried to make you fit the mould

. . . and cruelly judged you when you didn't get it right . . . and I promise to stop this blame game, starting now . . . I forgive you for all the times you didn't measure up to my impossibly harsh standards.'

Now open the chest, the armour, of the younger you and see and feel the presence of forgiveness and loving acceptance permeate the younger you.

While that is happening you might like to say, 'I'm so sorry for the past . . . and from now on I'm going to see the light in you, the love in you, the simplicity of grace that is your essence.'

And now imagine lifting the garment of pain and judgement off the shoulders of the younger you, taking that old coat of judgement and throwing it into the fire.

Now give the younger you some balloons. In the first balloon is self-love . . . Let the younger you breathe in self-love now, and let it suffuse and permeate the younger you . . . Now give a balloon of self-acceptance . . . Breathe that in . . . And a balloon of knowing you are the presence of divine being . . . Breathe that in and let it imbue and permeate the younger you.

Then imagine turning to the younger you and repeat the words, 'I'm so sorry for all the previous pain and judgement . . . From now on I will love and protect you and begin opening into the extraordinary essence of grace which is our nature . . . You are a beautiful being, full of magnificence and truth.'

Then, hugging the younger you, let the younger you merge into the present-day you, growing up now in the embrace of self-acceptance, self-love and self-knowledge and in the realisation that you are grace itself and perfect just as you are.

Now, once again, allow awareness to expand spaciously in front . . . boundlessly behind . . . and openly to all sides . . . infinite below and spacious above and just rest as an open sky of all acceptance.

And when all parts of you are fully integrated and ready to begin living from this consciousness of freedom and self-acceptance, you'll find you'll be able to open your eyes and be present to the here and now.

So when you are ready, you may open your eyes now and rest in a bath of self-acceptance.

honouring & reverence

Honouring and reverence –
the wings of grace.
With them you
soar blissfully in freedom.

Reverence is a fragrance of grace that arises only in all innocence and complete freshness.

Reverence is not a word that immediately comes to mind in the context of freedom, and yet, when you are resting in the presence of grace, you cannot help but feel a natural reverence for the magnificence of all creation shining around you. It arises spontaneously as the heart overflows with gratitude for the beauty of what is.

Yet this reverence is only available as a natural expression when you are fully *in this moment,* without any thought of the next moment and without any dragging of the past into the present. It is available when all comparison falls away and when all expectancy has dissolved.

I had a strong experience of this one balmy summer's eve on the island of Maui. The sun was just beginning to set as I stood on the docks having an idle conversation after what had been a long, lazy day on a boat that had listed and lulled a little too much for my tummy. Queasy and grateful to be standing on the stable surface of the docks, I was letting my body regain its equilibrium, as my friend Becky chatted away. She is a dear friend, whom I feel intimately sweet towards, so my attention was fully engaged, even as my body was finding its own inner balance.

As she spoke, a flash of orange light reflected off her sunglasses, and snapped me out of a somewhat sleepy lull, into a sharp awareness of that instant. I mentioned to Becky that some gorgeous apricot coloured light had just glinted off her glasses, and together we innocently turned to see where it originated from. There, on the horizon, the sun was getting ready to dip into the sea – a fiery, blazing red-orange ball. The sky was shot through with corally wisps of cloud, strewn across clear turquoise, which looked soft in comparison to the now deep watery-navy blue of the sea. A long, trailing orange glow reflected in the ocean, sparkling where it caught the tips of waves; creating a glistening ripple in the shimmering liquid light.

We both gasped. It took our breath away. Tears came spontaneously to my eyes as I stood in a reverie, lost in the moment, unable to speak. In silence, motionless, we watched the spectacular display of colours transmute into deeper and more intense hues, until finally the sun dipped fully behind the horizon and disappeared altogether.

An eternity took place. All was silent – just the gentle lapping of the sea as it slapped the docks and receded.

Turquoise faded into indigo, as a huge mellow moon appeared from somewhere, and a cool breeze wafted through. Everything became totally still.

My heart, overwhelmed with the glory, felt like it might not be able to hold such beauty. The immensity was too much. I felt I might burst with the exquisiteness. All reverence for life flooded consciousness – gratitude for what is . . . pure gratitude. Tears streamed down my cheeks. It felt as though we'd *always* stood on this dock, that we'd only ever been here – the moment lasted forever.

The next night I decided to go out to the same dock, hoping to experience the same magnificence, to taste the same true reverence, but sadly I found, try as I might, it just wasn't the same. Somehow, I was 'looking' for the same experience of the bliss of the previous night, but my very expectation, my longing prevented me from experiencing the simple, more subtle beauty that was shining everywhere on this sweet summer's evening. I kept calling to mind the previous night, remembering in detail the vivid colours and the spectacular display, and somehow this softer evening seemed pale in comparison. This night was a 'pastel' type evening and, lovely as it was, the moment seemed flat in relation to the night before. Somehow, the feeling of being graced just wasn't there; true reverence was missing.

Thinking that somehow I could call it forth and invoke it into existence, I closed my eyes. With all my being I pictured the previous night in all of its splendour. Hoping to feel the goose bumps that had come with the thrill of bliss wafting through, I only got a less heightened experience. Like looking at a picture in an old family album, it had all the right images, it just wasn't alive, fresh, new. I just couldn't *make* reverence happen.

There I was, standing on the docks, looking at a panorama of paradise, yet I couldn't see what was right there before my eyes, because I was too busy *comparing* it to my past experience. Seeing the moment through the filters of the past, I could only get a partially obscured view of the present.

I was *over*-looking the immensity of glory that was showing up right here, right now – showing up differently – with different colours, different clouds, different smells. But, because it did not match what I had come to believe was the ultimate sunset, I couldn't feel the natural omnipresence of grace surrounding me, and I left disappointed.

The next night, I ended up staring out to sea, *not expecting* anything. Grace had let me down. After all, it had only been a faded moment of glory, which disappeared into the sea – a fleeting glimpse of the divine. I turned my focus away from the ocean – it would only disappoint, after all – and let my toes sink into the sand. As the sun began to set, I noticed how the shadows lengthened and the sand quite suddenly grew cooler. A rough, broken shell was toying with my big toe and a bubble appeared in the sand, as the sea quietly snuck up on me and tickled my feet with its foam, then receded back into itself. Like a child, totally unexpectant, I lost myself in the tiny details of the moment, and a quiet, almost imperceptible bliss began to bubble up from somewhere inside. As I gazed at the sand, I noticed that the broken whitewashed shell was turning pink, and when innocently I turned my head to see the direction the glow had come from, I was arrested . . . the sun was just getting ready to set over the ocean, and the beauty took my breath away. My heart burst in gratitude and reverence, for the magnificence of life was everywhere.

Not wanting to compare, or cling, or memorise this moment in any way, I just rested in open reverence until the sun glided into the sea and disappeared.

It left me in a sweet stillness, and when I came home that night no talking was needed. This that had happened could not be spoken about, for I knew that in the describing I would have relegated it into the past. It would have become yet one more experience that had been labelled, and the very process of doing that would only take me out of the sweet stillness of the moment I was in.

Grace is like this. We cannot drag any previous thoughts, ideas or experiences into this moment and use them as comparison devices, for dragging in anything from the past obscures the grace and beauty of the moment that is here now.

It is only when, unguardedly, *all expectation is left out of the picture,* and all awareness falls on the now, that bliss, reverence, gratitude become the natural expression of the heart. It's when there is no movement to even *think* of the future, nor any desire to re-experience the past that all grace is here, all bliss is available, all reverence flows through.

In unguarded innocence, reverence is the natural expression of the heart.

It wasn't that any one sunset was better than the next. In fact, it wasn't the sunset that created bliss at all, for it is not what is seen, but *who is seeing* that makes the difference. The grace within you sees just this moment, and is awed at its own creation.

✲ ✲ ✲

When we are fully present, open to all creation, with no thought of either past or future, content with just *this*, all reverence arises as a natural expression of grace.

And when reverence arises, another fragrance of grace seems to accompany it: honouring. As soon as gratitude or appreciation for creation is here, a natural desire to honour, cherish and care for the beauty arises alongside it. It's as if they are two wings of the same bird. Reverence always inspires honouring; and when you honour and care for something deeply, reverence deepens. Reverence and honouring go hand in hand.

There is one story that is one of my personal favourites, as it pulls you into the power of honouring, and leaves you lost in simple gratitude and reverence. So once again you might like to settle in, relax and open to let this beautiful story do its work.

> There once was a woman who had grown very sloppy in her ways. She had gained weight, was feeling a secret, barely perceptible self-loathing, and had fallen into a mild depression. Without her noticing it was happening, her external environment began to reflect her internal dishevelment and dishonouring. She felt herself growing heavier, and found she really

didn't have the energy to pick up the growing clutter that was increasingly piling up around her. Magazines were stacked high around chairs, and the *Yellow Pages* lay open with maps and handwritten notes crumpled behind the sofa. Books never seemed to find their way back onto the shelves, and partially read newspapers were strewn about the place. Her not-fully-eaten take-away meals, which had left crumbs and stains all over the living room furniture, often didn't make it back into the kitchen for days, and television guides from the last several weeks littered the coffee table, covering the phone which had run out of battery, and which didn't ever ring much anyway.

There was no space to either walk or even place a dish *anywhere* in the lounge. In order to find a place to sit and eat, as she idly flipped through the television shopping channels, she would clear just enough of the previous take-away meals so she could put her latest containers down.

Her kitchen was piled high with dishes, but she figured, 'What's one more dish?' as she added another to the pile. The rubbish had grown too high for the bin, and needed to be emptied into a larger sack, but it all seemed too much of a hassle. As the flies were beginning to buzz around the kitchen, she kept the window open, to encourage the breeze to carry them away.

In her bedroom, her dirty worn clothes were dropped wherever convenient, and some lay on the bed. But as she felt more and more tired, when she went to bed at night she just pushed them to one side, creating only a small space for herself.

Upon rising, it all looked so overwhelming and, as there

wasn't a clean outfit anywhere, she decided not to change out of the clothes she had slept in. Fed up with the mess, she went back to the living room with her coffee, which she'd poured into a paper cup – easier than cleaning a glass or china mug – and began to peruse yesterday's newspaper.

As she paged through it, most of the articles didn't appeal. She'd already scoured for the more interesting bits, and she felt the urge to read something new, something fresh. It occurred to her that today's newspaper would likely be outside her door, but when she contemplated the effort it would take to find her slippers, unearth her dressing gown and surreptitiously scramble over the front lawn to get it before the neighbours saw her state of disarray, she got weary at the mere thought of it. So she turned her awareness back to the stale newspaper and with dissatisfaction continued looking for an editorial or article she might have overlooked the day before.

It was while she was in this quandary of whether to get up or stay put that she heard the doorbell ring. She looked at her clock up on the mantle. It was 11:32 a.m; who could be calling unexpectedly at this hour?

The doorbell rang again. Grudgingly, she went to her bedroom, finally found her bathrobe under a pile of clothes, and made her way to the front door. The person there, having patiently waited, but thinking that the doorbell must not be working, now knocked quietly on the door.

'Alright, alright. I'm coming,' she thought exasperatedly. – 'Like all I have to do all day is answer the door,' she grumbled.

When she opened the door, the bright morning sun dazzled her for a moment, and the stranger standing there, shadowed and silhouetted, was a bit hard to make out. There, in his hand, was a single white rose, and he spoke warmly, with the simple words, 'I brought this just for you,' as he gently placed it into her hand. As she looked down at the flower, she was puzzled and surprised, and a little bubble of gratitude arose from somewhere inside.

For a moment its beauty transfixed her. How long this moment lasted she did not know, but when she looked up to thank the kind stranger he was nowhere to be seen. Stealing her way a little further beyond the doorway, she peered in both directions to see where he had walked off to, but there was no one in her quiet, sleepy street. Somehow it was as if he had vanished into thin air.

Stunned and a little dazed by the light of the day and the experience of the unknown gentleman, she made her way back into the living room with her single white rose. Looking everywhere for a container to put it in, there was none to be found, so she went into the kitchen and found a small bud vase stashed in an unused back cupboard. She filled it with water, and got ready to put her rose into it, when she noticed that the vase was a little dusty. Not really thinking why, she gave it a good rinse clean, clipped the bottom of the rose's stem and put it into the vase.

She hadn't noticed it, but somehow she was walking with a little more energy in her step as she made her way back into the lounge to find a place on the coffee table for her new present. She moved a few magazines onto the floor, and found a spot right in the centre of the table to place her unexpected gift.

She sat down, and before she picked up her newspaper, she

took a moment to gaze intently at the flower so generously given her by someone she didn't even know. She began to notice its intricateness – the lushness of its petals, the greenness of its leaves, the texture and striations in the tightly held bud. She was surprised at its simplicity, and at its remarkable beauty. It was, after all, merely a simple white rose. Yet something about it seemed special. It crept under her guard.

When she opened her newspaper, still not having ventured far enough outside to pick up a fresh one, she found herself putting it down, so drawn was she to the beauty of her simple rose. As she looked at it, she became aware of all the clutter that surrounded it, and she thought, 'This rose is too beautiful to be sullied by all the mess around it,' and she quickly cleared off the coffee table, taking the rubbish right out to the big garbage bin in the back garden.

Again, she sat down to turn to the newspaper, but once again she found she could not take her eyes off the beautiful rose. It was exquisite.

Rapt in its beauty, her eye fell on all the clutter *surrounding* the coffee table. Oh my god. It's such a mess in here, she thought. This rose doesn't deserve to be surrounded by this filth. And with alacrity, mingled with a little disgust, the woman vigorously began to clear away all the rubble. She stacked the newspapers, organised the magazines, put the *Yellow Pages* back in a drawer and the books back on the shelf.

'Ah,' she sighed, 'there's more breathing space in here. Now, my beautiful rose has a place to flourish and bloom.'

The next morning, as she entered the living room, she stopped mid-stride. She'd forgotten all about the rose . . .

but there it was; its petals had begun to flower more fully – it was absolutely stunning. For a moment she held her breath; so exquisite was this unexpected sight.

As she stood there, she began to see all the crumbs on the carpet, and the stains on the upholstery, and the grimy film on the windows. They stood out like a sore thumb, in stark contrast to the pristine beauty of her immaculate rose.

'That rose is far too special, too divine to be surrounded by anything less than sparkling cleanliness,' said the woman to herself. She went straight to the broom cupboard, got out all her cleaning supplies and polished her living room until it was sparkling clean from top to bottom. She Windexed the windows, laundered the upholstery, polished all the wood surfaces and vacuumed the carpet. She dusted off each book and returned it to its shelf. She removed all the magazines, threw out all the newspapers and washed all the knick-knacks. She even rearranged the furniture, so that her exquisite rose would have plenty of room to breathe and expand in its beauty.

Finally, at four o'clock, she sat down to read a book that she had been meaning to read for many months, but as she opened to the introduction, she felt the book fall slack in her hands as, quietly, she grew still – lost in reverence at the beauty before her. How could so much beauty be allowed to be gifted to her? she wondered, as she basked in the glow of its radiance.

Sitting there mesmerised, she became aware of a smell wafting in from the kitchen. It was a slightly putrid smell and she started to feel restless. The pong was beginning to intrude upon and interfere with her simple enjoyment and appreciation of the rose. It was really starting to annoy her.

Not able to sit still another moment, she tore into the kitchen, and for the next several hours cleaned, scraped, scrubbed and disinfected that kitchen until it shone like sparkling crystal. The rubbish was taken out to the wheelie bin, the dishwasher washed the dishes squeaky clean, the pots and pans were polished to a high gloss and the entire kitchen radiated shining cleanliness.

By now it was midnight, so she went back into the lounge, took one last grateful glance at her beloved rose, turned off the lights and fell into bed.

In the morning, when she went into the kitchen to make her first coffee of the day, she was dazzled by how much light was there. She'd forgotten what a sunny kitchen it was. And as she got ready to step onto the clean, tiled floor, she noticed that the bottom of her feet had become sticky from the night before, and she didn't want to bring that muckiness into her sparkling kitchen. So she turned on her heels and went straight into the bathroom to have a shower.

What a mess, she thought, as she stepped onto the bath-mat. I never noticed it was this dirty. Like a thunderstorm, she swept through the bathroom, scrubbing, washing and cleaning until everything dazzled with light, and she stepped into the shower and thoroughly scrubbed her own body, as if this was the shower of a lifetime. She took a loofah and scrubbed her skin until it was pink. She shampooed her hair twice, and put on her most fragrant conditioner. While she was towelling off, she sprayed herself with her freshest cologne, and finally slipped on her robe – which now seemed a bit stale compared to the pristineness surrounding her.

With steaming hot coffee, now poured into her favourite

mug, she found her way into the living room, to go sit with her beloved rose. It was no longer morning, but that didn't matter, for she felt fresh and clean, and could sit gazing contentedly at her rose for as long as she wished.

As she sat there, tears welled in her eyes. How did she ever get so lucky as to have such exquisite beauty gifted to her? She innocently thanked the rose, and found herself falling to her knees in gratitude for such beauty. Reverence for life flooded her being: gratitude for just this.

As she revelled there in awe, she felt she had never seen such exquisiteness in all her life. This rose must be divine in some way, she thought . . . Time passed. How much time she did not know, but the sun's rays began to cast long shadows in the room, so she figured that evening must be near.

She became aware that the robe she was wearing felt somehow inappropriate to its surroundings. Everything was so pristine, and it was not. Not wishing to disturb the rose with a stale energy, she thought, I'll just pop this into the washing machine, and while I'm at it I'll get my other whites and give them a wash too.

She went to her bedroom, and beheld what seemed like a horror. There were dirty clothes strewn everywhere. How was it she'd never noticed it before? The whole place looked like a hurricane had come through.

Disgusted and a little shocked at herself that she could have allowed things to get this far-gone, she hurriedly picked up every item. She had at least five loads gathered. She washed them all, and while the loads were being laundered, she emptied her entire closet. 'I'm sick of this outfit . . . I haven't worn this in years . . .' she mumbled to herself, as she stripped her wardrobe almost bare. 'It's all going to charity. I don't need it – it's dead wood hanging about, cluttering up the place.'

She stripped the bed, washed and ironed the bedclothes, and finally, when all was tidied, ironed and put away, she vacuumed, scrubbed and polished each surface.

The whole room sparkled. Somehow, it was midnight yet again, so she went to the living room, took one last grateful glance at her beautiful rose, and fell into sweet, clean, ironed white sheets. She slept deeply, soundly, without even dreaming.

The next morning when she arose, a soft warm glow was suffusing the bedroom, and she lightly jumped out of bed because she realised she had awoken just in time to witness the sunrise – something she had not done since she was a kid. The dawn was spectacular, and with a skip in her step she went to the kitchen, made her morning coffee adding a touch of cinnamon, just because she could, then sat down in the living room with her glorious rose.

The rose had come into full bloom. It was radiant, voluptuous and splendid. Once again, she got down on her hands and knees. She began by thanking the rose, and asked if there was anything more she could do to honour its beauty. She was flooded with gratitude, not knowing how to thank such beauty for finding its way into her life.

Standing up, she walked over to the window and opened it, allowing the cool morning air to bathe the rose in freshness, and quietly, not wanting to make any noise that would create a single ripple in the exquisite, radiant stillness, she sat back down to stare in open adoration.

She finally felt relaxed to bask in the beauty – she could totally surrender to it, drown in it; nothing else could draw her attention away. It was just her and her rose. Such simplicity, such completeness, so sublime.

Time passed in just this way – the woman adoring her rose; the rose radiating beauty, embracing her and enfolding her in its fragrance . . . basking in the embrace of sublime being.

The doorbell rang . . . and the woman, stunned for a moment out of her reverie, innocently padded her way to the front door. She didn't notice that her feet barely touched the floor – so light had her step become.

When she opened the door, as her eyes adjusted to the morning sun, she saw the concerned face of her next-door neighbour.

'Oh, hello Margaret. I'm sorry to bother you. I just wanted to check in to see if you were alright . . . There are three days' worth of newspapers on your front lawn and, as your car was still here I didn't know what to think. I wanted to make sure you were OK.'

'Oh, sorry to worry you,' she replied. 'Uh, . . . I've just been rather busy . . . No, actually I'm fine . . . Would you like to come in for a cup of tea?'

The neighbour nodded yes, and said that it would be lovely, but her gaze seemed puzzled, and she couldn't keep her eyes off Margaret. Stepping through the door, she finally came out with it.

'Margaret, I can't help notice how shiny you are . . . You

look absolutely radiant . . . I'm actually dazzled by your light . . . What *have* you done to yourself?' she spilled out with genuine incredulity. 'You look beautiful.'

Margaret, surprised by the compliment and realising that her neighbour was as surprised as she was, and that the remark was completely sincere, was not quite sure how to respond. She hesitated, then stammered, 'Oh, no, no, Karen – you must be mistaken. You must be sensing the beauty of this white rose I was recently given. It's so radiant, you must feel its presence, even from here. Come into my living room, you won't believe how exquisite it is.'

Together they walked into the lounge, and stood admiring the rose. Karen kept looking from the rose to Margaret, from Margaret back to the rose. The silence became awkward. 'No, Margaret. *You* are mistaken. It's not the rose – it's *you*. Your light is making that rose look even more stunning, but it is pale in comparison to your radiance. You shine like the sun. This rose has become beautiful in your radiant presence.'

Stunned, not knowing what to say, Margaret went over to the mirror in the hall. The face reflected there was one she'd never seen before – it radiated beauty; it shone like the sun.

And, in that moment, she realised the extreme power of reverence. All she'd done was honour that rose, cherish it, care for it, make its life blessed, and in the process she too had become sacred. She too had been blessed. She too had become radiant.

When you truly revere life you are prompted by the deepest part of you to honour it. In the humble honouring, you become honoured.

In your blessing, you become blessed. In your loving, you become love.

Honouring and reverence: two wings of the same bird. You can't have one without the other, and with them both you soar on the wings of grace.

* * *

Invitation – Honouring and Reverence

Is there some aspect of your life that you have been treating casually; letting it become stale or unused? Or have you let something atrophy through lack of care, perhaps even letting it fall into disrepair?

Start by examining the material things in your life. Go through your home with a fine toothcomb: go into every closet, cabinet and drawer. Anything that you are not currently using and do not plan to use in the near future, should go. This is your invitation to let it go to someone else who could make good use of it. It's time to offer it to a friend, loved one or charity shop. Clean every cupboard, closet, storeroom – leaving only what you really, truly love, cherish and use frequently. Be willing to be ruthless. Be honest and clear with yourself: if you're not sure, let it go.

Next, check your clothes and shoes. Anything that doesn't fit; anything you don't wear from time to time needs to go. Those old Christmas or birthday presents you never liked in the first place – out they go. Those outfits you loved in the store, but hated as soon as you brought them home – sling them. Again, be ruthless.

Next, go through your bathroom cupboards and shelves. Toothpaste tubes, squeezed out, but not yet dumped – chuck them. Out-of-date prescriptions, perfumes that have gone stale, creams that are two years past their sell-by date – toss them.

Check your kitchen: is there an extra set of dishes you don't really use? Do you have two versions of the same pan, and only use the newer one? What about old, cracked or chipped mugs and cups? Be willing to be ruthless with yourself once more. Keep only what you love, and give away the rest.

Now, once you've cleared out all the extraneous clutter, go back to the items you *do* love. Do any need washing, repairing, dry cleaning, ironing, fixing, altering? How can you *really* honour them and bring them into shining condition?

Do whatever you can over the next week to completely restore every item, be it clothing, computers, vacuum cleaners, appliances, ornaments – be willing to invest the time to bring them into top condition. Make sure everything sparkles and radiates newness and care.

Then do the same with your house or apartment. Spring clean it until it shines. Clean carpets, furniture, windows, counters, drawers, and shelves – even closets and garages. Let your whole house shine from the inside out. Really honour it, respect it. Turn each item over and recognise the blessing it is in your life. Really honour that blessing.

In your honouring, a deep reverence may arise – a reverence for the beauty, the magnificence, for the blessedness of all life.

Next go to yourself: is there some way you are treating yourself casually – neglecting your health, skipping meals, avoiding exercise? Do you miss out on pampering yourself? Are you thoughtless in the way you groom or clothe yourself?

Well, start with a good shower and as you soap yourself down, realise what a blessing it is that you have arms, legs, a body with which to experience life. As you wash your hair, realise how fortunate you are to have good shampoo and conditioners. Realise that you deserve the finest.

Then, when you get ready to eat: if you were truly honouring yourself, what would you choose to put into your body? How would you exercise this beloved body and, if you were deeply honouring, how much time would you give yourself to meditate, contemplate or be still? And if you were dressing God for this occasion, how would you dress the divine self?

In honouring yourself, you might like to treat yourself to some fun – perhaps in nature – or some inspiring entertainment. Experience honouring and respecting yourself *fully*. It is a choice available in each moment.

Then, next week, or whenever it feels appropriate, sooner if you like, you might like to do the same with your relationships. Contemplate how blessed you are to have that person in your life. *Do* something to actively honour them. Take time to praise them, both inwardly and outwardly. You might like to make a list of all the qualities you admire or appreciate in them. Open yourself to how lucky you are to have other souls who care for you in your life, and lavish your partner or loved one or friend with great care. Just *choose* to honour them, even if only for one night. Experience the power of honouring, appreciating, and feel the gratitude that floods through when you actively honour and respect your loved ones.

Then, consciously choose to let this honouring and reverence overflow into the rest of your life. *Take* time out to truly savour the moment and the tiny nuances of the present. Just *be* still, present in the moment, open to what *is*.

✲ ✲ ✲

Honouring is a choice. And when you choose it, reverence follows in its wake. Your realise how sacred this that you are honouring is. In that, you are humbled, awed and left in a flood of gratitude.

There is a huge power in honouring what is. One moment spent in honouring floods your being with gratitude. Then *you* feel honoured, graced, filled with joy.

The more you honour life, the more you feel graced. The more you are graced, the more reverence you feel. The more reverence you feel, the more deeply you open and the more completely you give yourself into honouring. And so it goes . . . honouring begets reverence and gratitude, and they in turn beget a deeper honouring and grace.

And the beauty of it is that it is all available in *every* moment. Even if you stop right now and spend a few minutes just to honour, cherish and respect what is here, you will feel the murmuring of reverence bubbling up from within.

The choice is yours – and grace loves you so much that it makes that choice available in each and every moment.

Honouring and reverence –
the wings of grace.
With them you
soar blissfully in freedom.

emotions

If you open into the core of
any emotion, there you will find
the peace you are seeking.

Emotions are your greatest friends.
They are the gateway to your soul.

When I arose this morning and felt a compelling pull to write about emotions in the context of freedom I was quite surprised, but soon it became clear why our feelings had to be discussed when speaking about the boundless presence of the infinite.

We so often have the misconception that our emotions interfere with our experience of ultimate peace: that they are the storm that distracts us from the spacious calm. They *seem* to limit our experience of freedom and obscure the boundless field of grace, which by nature is vast, free and emotion*less*.

There are so many false notions about emotions. In some traditions they teach the value of *transcending* emotions; as if they are the 'bad guys' that hinder our experience of the divine. We are trained to believe that enlightenment is what happens when we have become *free* from our emotions, as if emotions are the captors that imprison us in the illusion of life.

Even if we've not been introduced to such concepts as transcendence and non-attachment, we still learnt at an early age that there were 'good' emotions and 'bad' emotions. If we were crying about something before going to school, mummy was quick to shut us up, and shut those 'bad' emotions down with a, 'Come on dear, dry your tears. It's time to go to school. Chin up . . .'

So from early childhood we learnt that 'bad' emotions weren't welcome and that only 'good' ones were allowed. If we felt fearful, shameful, hurt or angry, we were taught to cover it all up, push through and be strong. Those 'bad' feelings would only make us appear a wimp to the rest of the world, and a sissy to those more strong than us.

Pretty soon, *any* strong emotion arising caused an instantaneous shut down, and cover up, as we quickly tried to transmute it into something more comfortable to society. Even if we secretly sequestered ourselves away, hiding in our bedrooms to allow ourselves a few private moments to be with the emotion, we would often fight back the tears, try to talk ourselves out of what we were feeling or diminish its importance, and maybe even felt ashamed of our weakness in the process.

Emotions became our invitation to go to battle. The instant anything arose that we or society felt was too emotional, all our strategies to annihilate, deny, or transmute it arose . . . we fought it, resisted it, tried to explain it away; we argued with it, projected it and blamed others for it, blamed ourselves for feeling it, and ultimately started to develop more long-term strategies for suppression. We took up smoking, drinking alcohol, overeating, senseless television watching, endless reading of just about anything; all in an effort to narcotise and put to sleep any and all so-called unacceptable emotions that might dare to raise their heads and try to destroy our peace, or rob us of our self-acceptance or the larger acceptance of society.

Emotions became the culprits to be destroyed before they destroyed us.

It was almost as if some terrible devil called emotions lurked within each of our beings, and our job was to quell them, oust them, subdue them, get rid of them, push them back into the recesses of our consciousness – back into oblivion, where they belong.

In some spiritual traditions, they ask you to repeat mantras or incantations any time a 'negative' emotion arises – to avoid its ill effects, and keep your attention on the supreme. And in other traditions, aspirants submit themselves to extreme austerities and self-deprivations – braving the elements, chastising the body, undergoing fasts – they punish their bodies for being impure vessels, which gave rise to these 'bad' emotions.

Some yogis meditate in caves for years, so they won't be required by life to engage in any activity that might cause emotion to arise: that way they aren't plagued by these 'worldly demons.' And some western religions have confessional booths, or testimonials to congregations, so that one can confess the sins of having experienced an unholy feeling or an impure impulse. You may then be given a series of tasks, the difficulty of which is dictated by how bad your emotion or impulse was, to absolve yourself of your sin.

In nearly every spiritual tradition there is some reference to the need to obliviate or conquer the natural expression of human feeling; and those rare beings who seem to have successfully purified themselves of their impure and unholy emotions are celebrated as saints, or holy ones.

Indeed, everywhere we look, in every context of society, secular or religious, it seems that all of life is conspiring to kill our emotions, to suppress our natural feelings. It seems nearly everyone agrees with the culturally conditioned belief that most emotions are bad and must be subdued at all costs.

It's no wonder we can't experience peace for any length of time. We are always on the battlefield, fighting wars against the enemy – an enemy that won't give us any rest, for as soon as we quell one regiment, the next surge of emotion comes marching behind it, in an endless stream of never-ending waves. It's a battle we all fight, even though we know it's one we will never win.

For as long as we have breath in our bodies, and have life in our being, emotions will come as a natural part of being human.

It's as if we are fighting our very selves, our own nature. And what a fruitless, endless battle it is. It's exhausting. It's as ineffective as standing on the shore and holding up a shield against a tidal wave. Nothing you can do can stop its force, and any resistance only drains your energy and exhausts your being.

In fact, it is our very struggle *against* feeling that robs us of our peace, and disturbs our wellbeing. When so much effort is wasted trying to resist the natural flow of life, there is not much life force left to experience the inherent joy of life.

We are always on the battlefield, always at war: at war with ourselves. And it's our very resistance to what *is* that destroys our peace, robs us of fulfilment – not the 'negative' emotion itself, but the struggle *against* it; not the feeling, but the ferocity of our will to kill it.

We have become warriors: warriors fighting a phantom enemy called emotion. And when the battle becomes too much we collapse into depression, into a place of numbness, where the acute pain of the fight cannot reach us; and we seek counsellors to help explain our way out of the war zone, or doctors and psychiatrists who prescribe drugs to block out our intense feelings. Or we engage in pointless and mind-numbing activities to distract us from our feelings: we zone out watching vacuous television game shows, we wash the car or hoover the carpets when they're already clean, we gamble, we chatter and gossip endlessly about other people's problems – all in a game of emotional avoidance. Or we temporarily raise the white flag and plead for mercy: we turn to God and start to pray, seeking respite, or we go to an enlightened master and learn to meditate or to recite mantras. At best, we get a short window of peace before the next battle begins.

It never occurs to us to drop the role of warrior; to cease the battle altogether.

Maybe we all just need a change of profession. Maybe we weren't cut out to be soldiers in battle, fighting against life. It's just that no one ever gave us another job opportunity – they didn't offer us an alternative choice. Upon birth, society simply said, 'Oh, another warrior has arrived. Here child, take up your armour and shield like a good little soldier. Life is a battlefield, and though you'll never win the war your job is to fight the tide of emotions, no matter what. If you make some inroads we'll give you a medal of honour. If you succumb to weakness we'll ostracise you. It's an impossible job, but those are the rules. Keep up a brave face. Now march on, young one, march on.'

But what if you decided *not* to play the game of war? What if you finally said, 'No, I don't want to be a marine. I never signed up for the army in the first place.' What then? What if you gave up all resistance? What if you simply refused to fight?

What if, instead, you said, 'Come one, come all. All of my emotions are welcome into the ocean of love that is always here?' What if, instead of a battlefield, it was discovered that life is an infinite field – a field of trust, openness, love?

And what if, in this infinite field, all the natural flow of life's feelings were free to come and go? What if you provided no resistance whatsoever to the natural flow of life? I wonder what would happen?

That which you resist persists.

Your resistance to emotion is perpetuating the very thing you wish was not there. It's in the moment of true surrender, openness and acceptance that your emotions feel so welcome that they easily come, and just as easily go. Resistance keeps your emotions in play, and creates only more of itself. Resistance begets resistance.

It's time to call off the fight and welcome your enemy with open arms. When you put down your weapons, lay down your shield of protection, and look this so-called 'enemy' in the eyes, you will see yourself shining there; for there is no difference between you. There before you is the most human of human beings. You are looking into the eyes of a friend, and that friend is your Self.

The invitation is to finally lay down your arms, dear one, and welcome all of life with all your heart. Your old enemy will turn out to be your closest friend, and the only enemy still at large will be realised to be resistance itself.

The time has come to befriend your emotions. They are the gateway to your Self.

Let's examine our emotions . . . Just what are they? . . . Allow a feeling to give rise to itself right now . . . any emotion . . . If you are really welcoming, you will discover that it can arise quite easily. But what is it? . . . It is actually just a simple sensation in the body. Some of these sensations are comfortable and pleasant, and some are uncomfortable, but they are all ultimately just a bunch of physical responses to chemicals flooding through the body. And we can either resist the flow, or welcome it and allow it to flow through.

If we choose to resist or suppress the feeling, it only gets driven deeper into our subconscious, and comes up more intensely later on.

However, if we welcome it, it is free to rise, be fully felt and to subside naturally. And as long as we don't engage in any story about it, or stir up any drama about it; as long as we just let it arise completely, purely, without examination or analysis, then it will simply be felt and then dissolve back into consciousness. In this way it doesn't get driven anywhere or stored anywhere. These are the emotions that feel so welcomed, they feel so free that they just dissolve in the bath of love provided, and they don't bother to habitually revisit us.

It is our very resistance that keeps emotions at bay, waiting in the wings for the chance to come back on stage to be fully experienced.

In freedom, the embrace of love provides no resistance. It just says, 'Come emotion, you are so welcome. I've fought you long enough – now you are free to be fully felt.' When this happens, the emotion feels so embraced by your love that it arises and subsides naturally, like the ebb and flow of the tide.

Have you ever sat and watched an infant playing in a playpen? It will be sitting there, completely content, just resting in some sweet innocence of being. Then, some strong emotion might come flooding into its consciousness, and the child provides no resistance to it – it just openly and freely experiences it. Seemingly out of nowhere, you'll see joy come through, apparently for no reason whatsoever. The baby will laugh, gurgle, splutter and giggle, as the wave of causeless happiness courses through consciousness. Then, the next moment discomfiture may arise: the infant may screw up its face, pout its mouth, clench its fists and even pound against the rails of the playpen. This too will pass, and once again the infant will just rest in open-eyed awareness. Soon, it may notice a mobile floating playfully above its head and get lost in complete wonder. And that will subside as, once again, it will be resting in open beingness. Next, it may feel an urge to reach for something beyond its grasp outside the pen, and start to make noises of exertion and frustration in its effort to get to it. It might even cry in abject frustration, but eventually, this too melts away, and once again it is left hanging out in open presence.

The whole palette of human emotion comes to dance through the infant's consciousness but, because it has not yet learned that it is *supposed to resist* emotions (it has not yet been given its battle armour) it just innocently rests and lets the natural feelings flood through consciousness. Ultimately, the child is untouched by any of it. The emotion doesn't stick anywhere, because there is no resistance to it. Like a spring tide, it rises fully, is felt in its totality, then subsides and recedes. The infant's essence, its being hasn't been affected or changed in any way. It remains wide open and free.

Unfortunately though, once we begin to understand the meaning of their words, our parents embark on the huge project of instructing us in the way of the emotional warrior, and we begin to learn how to suppress, subdue, narcotise and deny these simple, natural feelings coming through our consciousness.

I wonder what would happen if we provided *no* resistance? . . . Would our essence be touched in any way by what came through it?

So often, I hear adults say, 'I feel so disconnected from myself. I just can't seem to access the *real* me. I've heard that there is a huge potential inside all of us, but somehow it eludes me. I sense it's there; I just don't know how to get past the blocks inside. I don't know how to find it.'

Of course they don't! They've lost sight of the infinite Self, of their essence – they're out of touch with their own hearts because they've spent a lifetime on the battlefield, *denying* the feelings that are the natural expression of their own essence. If they deny that expression, they deny *themselves*. They lose touch with themselves, and feel separate, bereft, alone, distanced, numb and disconnected.

And yet, every time an emotion arises it's presenting an open invitation to experience your Self. It is offering a doorway to your own essence, a gateway to your soul.

The very thing we have been suppressing is actually a gateway back to ourselves, to enlightenment, to freedom. We've closed the door on emotion, and in doing so we lost sight of our own essence.

Sometimes as adults we end up on an endless search to experience the divine, to find the truth of our own being, yet every time an emotion arises, we push it away. In so doing we push away the opportunity to open into the infinite. Our prayer was being answered but we ignored the response because it didn't come in the expected form.

This that you have come to fear and therefore subdue is, in fact, a gateway to your soul.

✲ ✲ ✲

Many years ago I had a huge, life-changing experience of this, which forever changed my relationship with emotions and ultimately provided an opening into the infinite that was so profound it gave birth to Journeywork – the original mind-body therapeutic healing work for which The Journey has become so well known.

Up until that extraordinary moment, I hadn't realised that *every* emotion is a potential opening into your Self. At best, I'd viewed emotions as a hassle to contend with. At worst, they were some huge obstacle to be cleared, released and let go of. But, never had I considered the possibility that they provided an entryway into my essence, a doorway into enlightenment.

I had not yet realised that emotions and enlightenment go hand in hand: until then, I believed the two worked against each other. But I've come to realise that every emotion is a gift. It's as if my own essence is reaching out with an open hand, inviting me into my Self. My emotions have become my best friends, and like any true friend they carry me into the best part of myself, into the love and wisdom inside.

Feelings are a priceless gift, which cannot be ignored. They are your invitation to come home to your Self.

I first discovered for myself the relationship between emotions and freedom when I was sitting with a group of about 150 seekers, in satsang with an awakened teacher in the early 1990s.

Having sat in meditation for several minutes bathing in stillness, we were just beginning the question and answer portion of the morning session. The stillness in the room was so palpable, it was like we were soaking in an ocean of it – it was everywhere, permeating everything. A middle-aged woman raised her hand and indicated that she had an urgent question regarding emotions. My ears pricked up as I wondered how the enlightened teacher would respond.

In the student's voice was clearly agitation and upset, 'I want to understand how you're supposed to feel all this peace when strong emotion is in the way . . . You know, I don't feel like all the rest of you . . . You all look so peaceful, so blissed out . . . I don't feel peace *at all*. I feel tormented. How am I supposed to feel all this so-called peace in the face of anguish?' she blurted out in anger, her voice dripping with sarcasm – almost blaming the teacher for her state.

The teacher looked her deeply in the eyes and said, 'Just don't move. Stay still . . . If you stay still and open right into the core of the emotion you are feeling, there you will find the peace you are seeking. Just stay still . . . Peace is there, waiting in the very centre of your torment.'

The woman seemed shocked, sceptical, and with a searing cynicism began to dispute the advice. The teacher remained completely at ease, politely waited until the woman had finished her sarcastic tirade, then with compassion simply repeated her previous instructions, finishing of with, 'Don't believe me . . . try it out for yourself. *You* discover what remains when all anguish has been welcomed. *You* discover what is there when you don't move away from the emotion, but just open *into it*, surrender into it, relax in it. Find out what is in the core of it . . . Try it out for yourself . . . Make an experiment of it . . . *just don't move.*'

The agitated woman initially seemed more interested in projecting blame at the teacher, but eventually settled down and must have decided to give it a try, to check out the teacher's words.

All the room remained patiently silent as we assumed she must have turned her focus inward, to follow the instructions she had been given. Her face, which had been contorted in anguish, hatred and projected blame, seemed to soften a little. Then it was as if hurt came fleeting across her face – out of nowhere. For a brief moment, she looked completely vulnerable, like a newborn – totally open.

Then I saw fear flash through her eyes; confusion, and inner scrambling seemed to be taking place. And I heard the teacher softly purr, 'Good . . . good . . . just keep opening . . . Go right into the heart of it . . .'

The woman looked up at the teacher for a moment, looking like she wanted to be saved from drowning, and for a second I thought she might lose her grip. She looked slightly terrified and out of control, as if she was trying to grab onto something and couldn't quite grasp it. Then, suddenly, her whole body relaxed and her whole face softened as relief poured through her. She began to breathe normally, easily, and a visible light began to radiate from what had been a hardened, harsh expression. Her face was now shining with beauty. She had an almost beatific expression.

I watched the whole incident in wonder. It was completely incomprehensible, yet there it was . . . somehow in the core of her worst emotion, she'd clearly found peace. She looked like peace, radiated peace, and her whole body was soft, pliant, her being open.

It had happened so fast.

After what could have been no more than two or three minutes, but which seemed endless, timeless, as we watched and waited with bated breath, she finally spoke – softly, incredulously, 'I get it . . . I get it.' She smiled, and tears poured down her cheeks. 'What a drama I'd created! There's so much peace . . . it's so easy . . . the peace was here all along.'

She began to laugh at some private, internal joke, then continued, 'Why did I make such hard work of it? Now I must look like all the rest of you bliss ninnies.' She laughed heartily at the irony of it. The teacher confirmed the truth of her comment, laughed, and finally the session turned to other topics.

When I saw the woman later in the morning session, she still looked radiant, shining like a cat that had secretly got the cream.

As I sat there for the remainder of the morning satsang, having carefully observed this remarkable scene, I felt increasingly confused and nonplussed. The teacher had given instructions that were the exact *opposite* of what everyone else out there was telling us to do.

In the 'real world', if you feel torment or anguish, doctors prescribe drugs so you don't have to feel it, and therapists endlessly analyse its meaning and significance trying to figure out how to get rid of it. If you consult NLP practitioners they try to reframe you out of it, so that it doesn't feel so bad. If you work with spiritual counsellors they try to find out which past life contributed to it, helping you put it into a larger, less painful context. If you go to bodywork therapists they try to help you release it, and if you attend emotional workshops they want to help you cathart it. Psychiatrists have it labelled, categorised and attributed to some early childhood event; hypnotherapists try to take you back through time to find out its deeper significance; and nutritionists attribute it to a chemical imbalance and get you to change your diet.

It seems that everyone has the same, certain belief – it's *bad* to feel that way, so let's *fix it*. And, even though they all have different ways to try to fix it, they are all convinced that fixing is the only way to peace and wholeness.

But this enlightened teacher was giving an entirely different, radical teaching. She was suggesting, 'No, no, *embrace* it . . . welcome it . . . love it so much that you surrender into it . . . go into the core of it . . . relax in it . . . and there, in the very essence of your worst emotions, you'll find peace.' And I had seen with my own eyes that this actually worked: that this hard-seeming woman had found peace and ease in the heart of her torment.

I began scrambling internally. Had everything I'd ever learned been wrong? Had we all fallen into the same huge societally driven hypnotic trance, where we'd come to accept that we had to get rid of these bad emotions no matter what? And, because of this culturally-accepted paradigm, had we all overlooked the obvious – the simple truth that if we really faced our emotions full on, felt them wholeheartedly, opened into the core of them . . . looked the tiger in the eye, and actually offered ourselves completely into it – that peace would always be discovered there? Could it be that the whole concept of fighting emotions was like fighting paper tigers, and that when we embraced them, welcomed them to be felt, they became our entry way into the infinite . . . that strong emotions were, in fact *good* things?

My being began to reel. Nothing made sense any more. Either the awakened teacher was out to lunch, or the whole world was so unhealthily conditioned that it didn't know up from down, or in from out.

I just couldn't accept what I'd seen with my own eyes. My *heart knew* that what I'd witnessed was authentic, real, true; but my mind was careening at the very thought that peace, or anything like it, could be found in the heart of our *worst* emotions. It didn't make sense . . . but there it was.

I simply couldn't take it at face value, so I decided I had to try it for myself; otherwise it would be only a passing memory of my perception of someone else's experience – and we all know how reliable memory is (not!).

So, I decided I would take some time to go into silent retreat and try the same experiment on myself. I simply had to find out if the whole world had gone mad and if in fact emotions were our key to enlightened awareness. I had to know it directly, as my own experience, not as some casual observation of someone else's realisation.

The fact was, it wasn't true unless it was true for *me*. And I simply had to find out the truth.

So, I told my husband that while he was away working I would take an at-home retreat: that I wanted to do an experiment to discover whether or not peace could truly be found in the core of our emotions. I explained that I would pick my most feared emotion, the one I was most hooked by, because only then could I be certain that the technique really worked.

So after he'd left I cleaned the house, changed the message on the answer machine, turned off the phone and sat down in a peach-coloured chair in our living room. I was going to try it, to find out if the whole thing was a lie, or bogus, or just a fluke – or whether it was true and we'd *all* been getting it wrong.

I sat there, holding onto the arms of the chair, not knowing what to expect. A sick foreboding feeling had been lurking in the background all day, as I prepared for the experiment, and now fear flooded my being. I didn't know if I had the courage to meet my worst emotion. It scared the dickens out of me. Tears flooded my eyes: I hadn't realised I would feel emotions this intensely.

I decided to meditate, to 'calm myself down,' but that made the fear come more strongly. It seemed unavoidable. Everywhere I looked, there it was. Finally, I mustered all my resolve to face it, be still in it, open into it, surrender into it; and I silently welcomed the fear.

For a moment I thought I might go insane with its ferocity, but I opened wider. Certainly, I had as much courage as that woman in satsang. If she could do it, so could I.

So I just gripped the chair as fear shook my being. I opened wider still and welcomed it, and just at the moment when I began to wonder if I could handle its intensity, something gave way inside. I let myself relax . . . my will caved in . . . I stopped resisting and just opened . . . I experienced a momentary relief and then, suddenly, loneliness. Sharp, abject loneliness was surrounding me. It was everywhere. It seemed impossibly strong, unbearable, but I'd made an agreement with myself that I would not move. I would stay open; I would welcome the emotion and go into the core, the very centre of it. So I said the word, 'welcome', albeit not too convincingly, and the loneliness became more pervasive. It seemed like the whole room was lonely: the walls were lonely, the chairs were lonely, I was lonely . . . everything was lonely, and there was no escaping it.

Something inside of me was still resisting, wishing to get out of this place, but I heard myself say internally, 'Relax, welcome . . . just be still in the face of the loneliness.'

Unexpectedly, my being responded and I did relax. Somehow, I felt myself opening and falling into a millisecond of relief, then plunging into a pool of despair.

Now despair was everywhere. I felt hopeless, helpless, pointless, worthless, useless . . . abject despair. I'd never known such despair in my life. It was searing and all consuming.

Part of me wanted out, to beg for mercy, but by then I had realised that the only way out was in. I knew I had to say the word 'welcome'. I knew I had to mean it, even if it meant being swallowed up by despair. I had to relax and give myself into it. Resistance was still lurking somewhere in my being, but I breathed into the despair, relaxed completely and let go.

For a moment I felt like I was dissolving, and then I became aware of being in the presence of something that seemed like a black hole, a vast field of nothingness.

Terror arose. What was this unknown empty field of nothingness? An inner scrambling began. The teacher hadn't said anything about a void, a black hole, an emptiness . . . no one had mentioned anything about anything like it.

The picture flashed of the woman looking like she was reaching out, trying to be saved from drowning: she must have felt like I did.

Terror was everywhere. I was terrified of falling into the black hole, terrified of being swallowed up into some emptiness. I thought I might go insane in there, lose myself, possibly even die.

I held on for dear life. I resisted with my whole being. I summoned all my will. I couldn't possibly let myself slip into oblivion, just fall into nothingness. I might not exist if I went in there.

Fear of dying flooded through. Fear of the unknown washed through. Fear of oblivion shook my being. I just couldn't surrender, not now – I might not exist!

I made my body rigid, I forced my mind into line – I kept repeating, 'Hold on, hold on. Don't let go . . . you know what happens . . . if you let go, you might fall into oblivion.'

And so I just sat there in my peach chair – absolutely stuck. *Stuck in resistance*.

I simply would not move.

After some time, the effort of resisting with all my might became exhausting. Sweat was streaming down my back. On the one hand I knew I had resolved to really stick this process out, and nothing could make me leave it, but on the other hand no one had said anything about a black hole or a vast emptiness. Could this be a big mistake? Was this really supposed to be here?

I tried to intensify my resolve not to give in, not to let go, but I could feel my will beginning to wane. I could feel it softening, and couldn't seem to muster up any more force to resist its pull to let go and relax.

Then I asked internally, 'What if you were never to leave this place of hovering over the black hole? What if you were to remain here throughout eternity?' And something inside shifted. The possibility of remaining frozen in terror seemed even worse than facing whatever was in that black hole of oblivion. Something began to give way. I felt myself relax, ever so slightly. I loosened my grip, and then, whoosh! . . . like a soft breeze, I felt my resolve melt, all at once. All resistance dissolved, all relaxation appeared, and as I let go into the blackness, I felt a peace softly pervading my being. As I relaxed even deeper, a lightness of being showed up and pure love flooded everything.

Everything became alive, as a scintillating presence of love shining everywhere. The presence was inescapable; it saturated, permeated the atmosphere. It was in the walls, chairs, and carpets, in the air, in me, in everything.

As my awareness began to naturally expand, I realised that the same presence was in the town I was in; it permeated the whole world, the entire universe. Inadvertently, I had dropped into a direct realisation of freedom, of infinite enlightenment, and I realised it to be a presence that was everywhere, in everything.

It wasn't some passing state of meditation, or just a momentary experience of peace. This was the direct realisation that who I was, was shining in everything: that I was the very stuff that made up the fabric of the universe – an infinite, eternal field of enlightenment.

Since that day, the realisation of who and what I am has never left. Every part of my being knows that I am totally *free* and part of *everything*. And yet, the whole drama, thoughts and emotions of life continue to play out – they just happen in the vaster context of this wholeness, this presence.

My emotions were not some bad things to exorcise from my being. They were, in fact, the gateway to my soul. And I realised that my soul is shining in everything, everywhere.

Each and every emotion you feel is the divine reaching out to you, beckoning you to let go, fall in and experience the boundless presence of freedom. The enlightenment you have been seeking is right here, in the very core of your worst emotions.

It's time to befriend your emotions, for they hold the key to the infinite, they are your route to your Self.

It's time to come home.

✡ ✡ ✡

Over the years since that time, my emotions have become a never-ending source of self-discovery.

I have now learned to open into them more easily; effortlessly breathing into any resistance, consciously opening, relaxing into the core of them, and I have developed many practical techniques for coaxing myself and helping others out of fighting and resisting. Much of the current elegant and facile quality of advanced Journey techniques is born out of having found dozens of ways to get resistance to relax, for the truth is the moment you *choose* to relax into the core of an emotion you drop through easily and open into the infinite.

For me personally the whole process can happen in as little as two minutes, and most often takes approximately five minutes. For others, when they first undergo the emotional drop-through process it often takes a little longer, because resisting what's here is such an ingrained habit. So we're trying to help the habit loosen its grip: we're needing to coax the old resistance into relaxation, trust and release.

But truthfully, once you get the hang of it, opening into your emotions, embracing them, relaxing into them, can become an easy process.

Children are amazing with Journeywork. They trust completely, and that is the key. They drop through their emotions into peace as effortlessly as milk being poured into brewed tea. Because there is no resistance with them, because they trust utterly, they fall into peace, happiness, joy as easily as a river flows into the ocean. There is no struggle for a young child.

It's only we adults who have come to worship struggle. We have come to idolise it. We receive medals for it. As a matter of fact, if something is easy or simple, it is considered insignificant, or insubstantial. So we've created a whole paradigm called, 'create resistance so that I have something to struggle with'. Then we can maintain our standing as a ranking officer in the emotional army.

The 'war against terrorism' has become a globally recognised phrase in recent years. I think the most pervasive war for many centuries has been 'the war against emotions'. It's a war we've *all* engaged in, and have foolishly come to believe in.

But the time has come to stop the war, call off the resistance and open your being into the infinite, the boundless love that is always here. Though we've long had this war against our emotions, there is also a way in which we've created a love-hate relationship with the same emotions we've been fighting against. We are totally transfixed by them.

We love to explore their meaning, obsess about who's to blame for them, dramatise about how we've been victimised by them, gossip to our friends about how bad they are. We go to counsellors to find out their origin, to workshops to bring them up and cathart them, and we entertain ourselves with endless mind talk about their significance in our lives. After all, who would we be without all this drama? It's what gives us our character, our colour, our reason for being. Emotions give us our identity . . . don't they?

One of the things I've found to be absolutely true about emotions is that they are essentially fleeting. Emotions come and go at the drop of a hat. They can't last for more than a few moments, *unless* we give them meaning, create a story around them, add our energy to them.

Without a story attached, emotions are just sensations that come and go. They have no more meaning than a bunch of chemicals flooding through the body. *However*, if we decide that they are significant, important, that they must be explored, analysed and understood: if we keep replaying the drama surrounding them, using our thoughts to enhance them – then we can keep emotions in play for as long as we want.

Emotions are just momentary sparks flickering in consciousness. However, if you pile on fuel adding the lighter fluid of a little drama, feeding the flame with your thoughts, and adding the newspaper of someone else's opinion; if you then fan this now roaring fire with gossip, or your therapist's opinion, you can really create a huge blazing bonfire out of them.

Of course, the fire will eventually burn out, naturally, of its own accord, *unless* you keep adding more fuel to it.

You probably have not been previously aware of your battle strategies but, as you are indeed fighting only a phantom enemy, you have to invest constant effort in propping up your notional adversary. You have to fan the flames of emotion so that you have something to do battle with, to struggle against, to resist. You are actually battling, fighting, subduing, and trying to oust an enemy that *you* alone keep alive with your thoughts, dramas and energy.

The fact is that, without your *story* of victimhood and blame, any emotion would be just that – a feeling wafting through consciousness. It requires your concentration and belief in your drama, your story in order to be kept alive.

So, what if you were to decide to stop the story . . . just drop it?

It's such a relief. Then, when pure emotion arises, you can recognise it as your friend, and with open arms welcome it, love it, relax in it and, ultimately, find freedom in the heart of it.

One of the paradigms that have become popular in recent times for ousting a 'bad' emotion is catharsis. And I can understand *why* that is so enticing. After a good cry, or a temper tantrum, we actually feel some temporary relief – and that is intoxicating. But it still doesn't *solve* the problem, because inevitably the emotion will come flooding again at another time.

So, what I recommend is no dispelling it, no acting it out, no analysis, no collapsing into it either; no fighting, struggling or even running from it – for it will surely eventually hunt you down and find you if you do. Rather, just turn and face the tiger directly, surrender and discover the love that's in its core. All other avoidances will only prolong your pain. You cannot run from your emotions. If it's peace you seek, your only effective option is to dive into them.

Relaxing, embracing, surrendering, trusting – these are the only tools of a lover of truth. So, turn from a warrior into a lover.

Emotions – they truly are your gateway to the infinite.

* * *

Guided Introspection – Emotions

Emotions are the entryway into the infinite. They are your route back to your Self, and they provide an easy access to the peace that is already there, calling you into your very essence.

You might like to start by finding a quiet space where you can sit without interruption for the next several minutes. You can put on the companion CD or perhaps have a friend read this to you so you can give yourself fully into your own internal process. If someone else is reading to you, just make sure they read it through a few times first so they are familiar with it, and get a sense of the pacing. Remember, . . . indicates a pause.

Begin with a prayer, or intention that you long to learn to embrace your emotions; to welcome them, to say 'yes' to them – and let your being know that everything is welcome to come up in this embrace. Even the hidden emotions, the tucked away and secret feelings, the unaddressed and unfamiliar ones are welcome. Put out the intention that even the emotions you've never acknowledged are welcome to come up.

Just sit quietly, let your being settle and let your awareness become vast and spacious . . . let it expand boundlessly in front . . . spaciously behind . . . and openly and freely to all sides . . . vast below . . . sky-like above . . . Just rest in an open sky of presence.

Make your heart as wide as the world . . . wide enough to include not just *your* emotions, but *all* emotions that exist . . . even wide enough to include your ancestors' emotions . . .

Really make the embrace of your love so wide that it can include all the suffering of humanity . . . Your love is that vast, and it is all-accepting, all embracing, all compassionate.

Now, specifically invite a personal emotion to give rise to itself within this embrace . . . really allow it to come up fully, innocently . . . with no need to change it, fix it or analyse it . . . j*ust welcome it*

Then, let your awareness go to the place in your body where it seems to grab you most strongly . . . Notice the sensation of it as it arises in your body . . .

Really surround that area of tension with your acceptance, your own love . . . With your whole being, let the emotion know that you are open to really *feeling* the sensation of it . . . the full power of it . . .

If you feel any resistance showing up anywhere, welcome that, too – it's natural, it's what we've been conditioned to do. But it's okay to feel even this, so bring your awareness to any resistance, and let it soften. You can let it know that it's safe to feel . . . the resistance does not need to protect you any more . . . You are allowed to fully feel *whatever* is here . . .

Be kind to yourself . . . opening into an emotion feels like the opening of a flower . . . you can't force it, you can only allow it, coax, welcome and provide space for it to bloom into fullness.

Let your feeling be allowed to bloom . . . let it become fuller still . . .

If an impulse to run away from, to avoid the emotion arises, recognise it, acknowledge it . . . know that this is natural . . . bless it and surround it with your loving awareness . . . then once again bring your awareness back to the original feeling . . . and allow it to be fully felt . . .

Our emotions can be quite timid at first . . . they are so used to being shut down, stamped out, ignored, run from . . . like rejected children, your feelings may not trust *you* at first . . . they may be shy with you . . . because in the past you've so often turned away from them . . .

So, now is your chance to turn towards your feeling . . . whatever it is . . . Welcome it with all your heart . . . You might apologise to it for having been so judgmental in the past . . . Really welcome it with every fibre of your being . . . Fully accept and embrace it . . . Good . . .

As the feeling grows stronger, just be curious to know what is there in the very heart of it . . . Feel yourself opening, relaxing and surrendering right into the very core of the emotion . . .

You don't have to fix it, change it or do anything . . . Just relax in the core of that emotion . . . Seek out any places that you may be resisting . . . soften them . . . and deeply relax . . .

What is here? . . . Good . . . Now, with the innocence of a child, feel yourself surrounding, opening, welcoming this emotion . . . allowing it fully . . . like a flower coming into full bloom . . . and then, with tender curiosity, feel what is in the core, the very centre of this *new* emotion . . . Feel yourself growing vaster . . . opening totally . . . and falling into, dissolving in, opening further into the core of it . . .

Just relax there . . . What is here? . . . Great . . .

(From time to time, with an emotion, you can ask what's behind it or beneath it.)

Continue opening in just this way, repeating the last paragraph of the introspection: as if you were gently lifting back the petals of a flower, and falling in naturally, effortlessly deeper.

At some point, a vast nothingness may appear, or a black open field or void of emptiness may show up. This too is just another petal. Just ask what is in the core of it, and relax and open and you will feel yourself dissolving through it as well.

Eventually, if your heart is open and your being relaxed and welcoming, you will find yourself basking, bathing, soaking in an ocean of peace, love, light, freedom: a boundless presence of grace will be surrounding you and suffusing you.

Just be silent and rest in this as long as you like . . . and you may open your eyes when you are ready.

The key to this process is to relax totally, be open and welcome fully whatever shows up. If any stories or dramas or memories come up regarding the emotion, please do not entertain them or let them distract you – for all images are merely a way for the mind to pull your focus away from the pure experience of the emotion. They are simply distracters trying to draw your awareness into some mind-game. Instead, let the memories or pictures go, as you notice the way they make you *feel* emotionally, and just stay open in the emotion . . . really welcome the *feeling* fully.

If a memory needs further attention and healing, you can always get *The Journey* book, and do a full Emotional Journey process to release the stored pain, and come into full forgiveness and complete understanding. But, for now, with this simple process, just let any images come and go, and let your full awareness be *in* the emotion you are feeling.

If at some point you feel like opening your eyes, there is no problem with stopping at any point in the process. All feelings can only last a few moments – they come and go as the natural ebb and flow of life. The vast, boundless presence that you are resting in remains untouched by the activity of emotions coming and going through it . . . No problem.

Just *know* that we are *all* in the baby step stage of learning to befriend, welcome and feel our emotions, and each time you do this simple process, you will feel more and more relaxed, open and easy.

It really is a process of learning to trust yourself. Over time, resistances will naturally melt away, as your being learns to trust you more and more.

You are a beautiful flower. It's time to open and let your exquisite magnificence shine. Emotions are your truest of friends. They are the gateway to your soul. They are part of the dance of enlightenment.

gratitude

Gratitude is the most immediate
and instantaneous way to
experience grace that I know of.

Grace simply cannot resist a grateful heart
and the moment you bring your awareness
to what you are most grateful for,
grace appears.

Gratitude and Grace
like two lovers they fall ever more deeply
in love with each other until they are lost
in each other, inseparable.

Gratitude is the most immediate and instantaneous way to experience grace that I know of.

It is said that gratitude magnetises grace. Like a bee with honey, grace cannot resist a grateful heart, and the moment you bring your awareness to what you are most grateful for, blessed with and appreciative of, grace immediately appears. I've begun to realise that they are inextricably linked. Gratitude draws grace, and when you experience the presence of grace embracing you, it evokes more gratitude. Like two lovers, they fall ever more deeply in love, becoming lost in one another.

Ultimately, there is no difference between the two, for to feel truly grateful is to know grace, and to experience grace is to feel blessed and grateful. It seems one cannot go anywhere without the other. These two lovers are too infatuated to be separated.

Of all the fragrances of the infinite that have followed me through the writing of this book, gratitude has been the one constant. Frequently, tears well in my eyes as I realise how lucky I am to be used as a vehicle of grace in the writing. I am overwhelmed by the tenderness surrounding me, the wisdom that arises, the joy and effortlessness of grace. I feel so blessed to be in its constant presence.

How can I help but fall to my knees to thank this infinite lover for its effulgent bounty. How can gratitude ever be enough to thank the ocean of grace?

Gratitude is available the instant you bring all your awareness to this moment, and really open your being to experience what is here. Even the simple swirling of smoke rising from a candle can evoke gratitude. When you take a moment just to *notice* what is around you – the beauty of a specific colour in the fabric of the chair you are sitting on; the grain of the wood on the table; the pristine clarity of the glass holding your drinking water; the variety of fragrances wafting through the open window; the angelic innocence in a baby's eyes; the joyful laughter of children playing in the distance; the fact that you have a roof over your head, or the abundance of having this book come into your hands – everything around you becomes a window into gratitude, an opening into grace. Even the food that nourishes your body and the padding footsteps around the house, signalling that you are surrounded by beings that care for you, evoke deep gratitude. And there is the unseen, the unknown, the stillness. An open heart cannot help but overflow with gratitude for this boundless presence.

Just bring your awareness to this moment and open your heart, your eyes, ears and being to *what is* already here, surrounding and embracing you. Every single experience in your life is an opportunity to fall into gratitude.

Gratitude is immediately here when you take time to open your heart to thank life for what is: for its blessedness, its beauty – for life itself.

In order for gratitude to be true and full there must be *total acceptance* of what is here in this moment – even if it doesn't show up in the usual, expected, accepted or obvious form that would normally invoke it. It's when you totally embrace and accept *what is,* without wishing to change it or fix it; when you totally allow life to be as it is, that gratitude overflows and grace is experienced as everywhere.

I remember having an uncanny experience of gratitude that was almost overwhelming in its force, in the most unlikely of circumstances. It arose from my total acceptance of what life presented, even though the outward appearances might have seemed utterly unfair and unacceptable.

It was about a year after the tumour healed. At that time we were living in a tiny cottage on the beach in Malibu, California. It was the autumn of 1993, and I had taken a couple of weeks to help my friend Elaine with a television episode she was directing in New York City.

Someone came into the studio and asked if anyone lived in the Los Angeles area, as a catastrophic forest fire was sweeping across and destroying tens of thousands of acres of land in the Santa Monica Mountains, along the coast of Malibu. He went on to explain that the fire was out of control, and that an 'all call' had gone out on national news for all neighbouring states to send in their fire fighters – that California couldn't handle it on its own. It had already been declared a national disaster.

When I first heard the news everything stopped for a moment. I held my breath and became keenly sharply present, totally aware. I said nothing. Elaine suggested it might be a good idea if I excused myself and went into the green room to get more details from the news, 'You need to find out if your house is in danger, Brandon.'

I went to the green room and was transfixed by the television screen. The fire was blazing seventy feet high, and was completely unmanageable. Fanned by very high winds it was spreading by miles every few minutes. As I watched my familiar coastline, I saw home after home of my dear friends get incinerated, completely wiped out in a seemingly miniscule space of time. It seemed impossible: I wasn't just watching some disaster movie – this was *real* life. And these weren't any old houses burning to the ground – they were the homes of loved ones being consumed by flames.

The smoke was too thick to see what was going on in the immediate vicinity of the coastal beach area where I lived, but my heart broke open for all those who had just lost their homes. I was aware that most residents in Malibu don't have home insurance, as it's too expensive. When you live on the coast in such a naturally volatile area you would need disaster insurance for violent storms, tidal waves and sea damage, earthquakes and fires – and the cost is astronomical. So my friends weren't just materially bereft, they were left financially devastated.

The next morning I got the news. For whatever reasons, the flames had unexpectedly leapt over the Pacific Coast Highway, and our little cottage had been consumed in a matter of minutes.

It was the only property on the beach side of the highway to burn down.

The fire fighters had been stationed directly outside our door in an attempt to stave off that possibility. They had already sprayed down the roof in an effort to prevent it from catching fire. But it simply wasn't the will of grace.

Even with all hoses poised at the ready, once the fire had started it was impossible to quell. The cottage burnt down like so many matchsticks. Our car exploded in the aftermath, and so nearly everything we owned and had gathered in our eighteen years of marriage and family life was gone.

At forty years of age with no insurance I would be starting life at the beginning again, without as much as a set of dishes or a winter coat to wear.

My husband, who had also been working away from home, picked me up at the airport and, as we drove together up the Pacific Coast Highway, I felt a growing dread gnawing in my guts. For the first time I was seeing the devastation up close. It was beyond anything I could have expected: so raw, so real – not some hazy image on a television screen. It was right there – the horror of it in my face, unavoidable. Every bush, tree, flower, plant had been scoured, and what remained were pitch-black ashes and burning embers, still smoking – a black moonscape dotted with an occasional house, sitting alone, somehow miraculously spared, but surrounded by a bleak wasteland.

As I gazed at it all, I became aware that there must be some reason why some homes were totally untouched, without a single scorch mark, while others had been razed completely to the ground.

It was as if some mysterious hand of God had reached in and totally spared this particular house or that specific building amidst an otherwise charcoal-blackened desert. And though I couldn't begin to fathom its mystery, I could sense there was grace running through it. It was so obvious, so apparent. It didn't look random at all. What the reason was – why some homes had been entirely spared, garden and all, while all their neighbours' houses had been totally devastated – I had no idea.

But the hand of grace was unmistakeable.

As this quiet realisation was dawning somewhere on the edge of my consciousness, an increasingly sick feeling of foreboding began to well up inside my body. The fear of what it might be like to *face* what *our* home looked like completely burnt out grew in my belly, getting stronger as the car got closer to our section of the coast.

My husband and I remained silent for the whole of the ride. As we came around the bend near our cottage, I summoned all courage, and quietly braced myself, expecting the worst. We were left speechless with the breadth and depth of the devastation before us.

Silently, we pulled up into our driveway. My husband turned off the ignition. Neither of us spoke: we just sat there staring.

My awareness was wide open. I wanted to take it all in – to really see it, to face it directly. All of my being became fully present, sharp. I was keenly aware, and riveted into the moment. As I looked, I saw the steaming remains of a hollowed-out façade, and beyond the blackened, burnt-out embers was a clear blue sky above the shimmering ocean. The pitch-black beams created a stark silhouette against the vivid cerulean vista beyond.

There was something strangely beautiful about it. There was life, in all her magnificence: all devastation, all glory, side by side in one stunning, dazzling view.

Tears began to well up: tears of gratitude. Gratitude for the beauty of life, for the magnificence of creation, for the mystery, for not knowing anything – gratitude to be alive, to be allowed to experience just this moment. All gratitude flooded, and my heart burst wide open.

I turned to my husband and said, 'It's amazing how much better you can see the ocean, now that there are no walls here.' He smiled ironically, and nodded agreement. He too was lost in a moment of complete awe.

We'd dropped all expectation as to how it was *supposed* to look, and had somehow totally, completely and utterly accepted that what was before us was simply what *was*. No wishing it was different, no efforting to change it, no asking, 'Why me? Why this house? Why was *our* home the *only* one on the beach to burn down?' Nothing but pure acceptance.

And in all acceptance, gratitude arose naturally, of its own accord. And with gratitude, of course, grace quickly came flooding in behind it. I felt embraced in grace, suffused with it . . . and because of it, somehow, I was the luckiest person alive.

We began to pick through the rubble, digging here and there to see if we could find a memento, some piece of memorabilia; something that would serve as a memory of eighteen years of marriage. As I looked at the charred, melted bits of appliances, broken pottery, smashed glassware, soaked half-burnt books – everything began to fade into insignificance.

It was just *stuff*.

I became aware of a huge love that was embracing me, that seemed wholly untouched by any of the leave-taking of items. It was scintillating as a vast presence in everything – with or without the accumulated material effects of family life. Something essential remained – my *self*. Somehow, the love seemed even more apparent, more exposed, more expansive when all the trappings of life had fallen away.

It wasn't at all what I expected to feel. Yet, there it was, as plain as day. I wasn't doing a Pollyanna snow job, trying to deny the truth of my real emotions, nor was I trying to reframe what was taking place and create a more positive frame of mind. The simple reality was, when I opened fully, in complete acceptance of what was there, I realised that I was no less whole – nothing had been subtracted or taken from the real, essential me.

All that remained was love. I felt an overwhelming gratitude for this love, gratitude for *being* love, gratitude for the love in my marriage, gratitude for life itself. This love could not be marred, lessened or altered just because my stuff was gone.

Even when I came across a dented, barely recognisable souvenir from a beautiful holiday, for a moment I felt a sweet recollection of that time, then a gentle letting go. And I realised that the item would never capture the joy we shared as a family, and that the memory would always be in my heart. I remember picking up a piece of jewellery, wondering if I could salvage it. It had both monetary and sentimental value, and I held out the hope that it could be fixed. But as I held it in my hand it just grew heavy, empty. It was nothing more than a bit of matter: it seemed dead compared to the shimmering, alive grace I was resting in. After sifting through all the rubble, ultimately, the only real things that remained were love and gratitude.

Over the next year, part of my learning was to accept whatever grace offered, no matter what form it came in. Someone would give me their old sweatshirt, someone else an unused mattress that had been sitting in their garage. Some gave me their out-of-date spiritual texts, and others offered me a vase or their second set of dishes. Grace was hugely, beneficently generous. Part of my dharma was to accept with an open, grateful heart and with both hands. And I began to realise that it was gratitude for life that had prompted people to share their abundance with me. It was a vehicle through which grace could express itself. In their giving, everyone was graced; in their offering everyone was blessed.

The ebb and flow of gratitude and grace: two inseparable lovers who come to dance in the embrace of acceptance.

* * *

Guided Introspection – Gratitude

'More is added unto the one with gratitude.'

I'd really love for you to get a direct, visceral experience of just how powerful a thankful heart is: how it is almost impossible to resist, and how it naturally draws abundance to itself.

So, take a nice deep breath in . . . and slowly let it out . . . and another deep breath in . . . and slowly breathe it out . . . And, as you read this story, imagine that it is actually happening – feel what it really feels like to experience these two similar scenarios, as if you are the key player.

Imagine that you are living in a lovely seaside village, and that the two houses on either side of you became available for sale at the same time. Two new neighbours move in during the same week, and you are eager and curious to get to know them. You give them a couple of weeks to settle in, and you wait for an appropriate natural time to introduce yourself. One morning, you spot the neighbour on the left-hand side mowing the lawn and you decide to seize the opportunity to say hello and welcome her to the neighbourhood.

After the polite niceties are over, you enquire as to how she is getting on . . . how she is settling in, how she likes the area and what her experience of it is. After a slight hesitation the neighbour responds rather downheartedly, 'Well, I moved here because I got a great job . . . my dream job, actually . . . and I was really looking forward to getting to know the area. But, I have to admit, being from the city I didn't realise it would be such a stretch to live in a smaller town . . . Don't get me wrong, the people here seem nice enough . . . it's just that it's not what I expected, I suppose. The neighbours across the way pointed my husband and me to some beautiful cliff walks, but I didn't have the heart to tell them that it doesn't really interest me . . . I have to admit the air is cleaner and healthier here, but I'm not really an outdoor person . . . I mean, mowing the lawn is not really my kind of thing. And I don't much like insects . . . or some of the animals around here – like that dog across the street: it keeps bounding into our garden like it owns the place and tries to lick me whenever I shoo it away . . . I've never been much of a dog lover . . . I feel totally invaded . . . And, truthfully, I'm not used to having such close contact with people as seems the way around here . . . It's so personal . . . I mean, in the city everyone minds their own business and we just get on with things . . . It's a nice enough place, this, and I suppose many people may love the idea that it's got great sea views . . . but I'm not into sailing or swimming . . . or anything rugged for that matter . . . it's kind of wasted on me . . . and now I've bought the house and I'm stuck here . . . I know prices have gone up since we bought, and that it's already been a great investment . . . but I really think I've made a mistake coming here at all.'

The conversation winds down. You politely excuse yourself and go back to your house.

Now check yourself. How are you genuinely feeling? Are you feeling somewhat flattened or drained? Check inside – do you feel any generosity towards your new neighbour? Do you feel keen to help and support her, or not? Do you feel drawn to her . . . or mildly repelled? Just check your being . . . Is there some contraction here?

Now experience the rest of the same story.

The next day, you see your other neighbour on the right-hand side, in the garden, digging weeds in the flowerbed. You introduce yourself, and ask how she's getting along; how she likes the area . . . and before you can finish your question your neighbour excitedly finishes it for you, adding . . . 'Oh, I'm so grateful to meet you . . . I just *love* the area . . . I feel so blessed just to be here. You see, I come from the city, and though I'm more used to an anonymous life on the go, I really love the freedom I feel here. The sea air is so sweet, so refreshing, and I don't have to tell you how staggering the views are. And that neighbour's dog that comes bounding into my garden and licks me every time he sees me . . . he's so friendly . . . I've never been much of an animal person, but he's won me over hands down . . . And this probably seems stupid to you, but this is the first time I've actually got my hands dirty tilling soil . . . Can you believe it? . . . I'm actually weeding and planting flowers. I didn't realise how rewarding that would be . . . And the neighbours . . . they're so friendly, so helpful . . . they suggested I take this cliff walk and I took them up on their offer . . . My God, I'm not sure I've ever seen such beauty, especially on a rainy, bracing day. It blew me away . . . I can't wait for summer . . . I'm not really the nautical type, but I'd love to give sailing a go, the yachts look so amazing . . . I didn't really expect to have this response to this place . . . coming from the city, I thought I'd be bored . . . but I've come to realise that the city seems dead compared to the aliveness of the life in a country village. I really enjoy getting to know people personally – I don't feel so detached . . . it's like I'm part of a community . . . And this is all on top of having come here because I got offered my dream job with a great company in an area where property price increases have already made my house a great investment. I work at the same place as that woman on the other side of you . . . Have you met her yet? . . . I don't know how I came to be so lucky . . . I'm just so grateful . . . I feel so blessed.'

You smile, let her know you need to go run some errands, and turn to go back into your house.

Now, once again, stop and check yourself. How are you feeling towards this neighbour? Do you feel inspired, blessed, grateful to have met her? Is there a feeling of wanting to shower her with more of what she is so grateful for, or in some way give her support? Are you already thinking of other sights and areas in the vicinity to introduce her to? Are you feeling like you want to enhance her experience? Do you feel even more grateful to be living in this village yourself?

Take a moment to compare your responses. Both neighbours were genuinely polite to you. They both live in your seaside village, with the same views, with the same neighbours with the same dogs – yet their responses were very different. One came to you with a cup half empty, whereas the other's cup was overflowing with humble gratitude. Which did you feel more drawn to?

When someone is grateful – isn't it true? – you want to give them *more* of what they are grateful for. Life cannot resist a grateful heart. And when we approach life with a cup half full, instead of half empty, life starts to shower us in abundance.

A grateful heart tends to beget more of what it is grateful for – because gratitude is a magnet.

In contrast, an ungrateful heart tends to spiral itself down into a sea of lack and scarcity, and soon all that's experienced is what is *not* there, what is lacking, what is missing. When we focus on lack we create more of it. When we focus on how blessed we are, we tend to draw more blessings to us.

It may seem to be a very simple principle, but it is extremely powerful. If you are honest with yourself, how often do *you* choose to practice thankfulness? Gratitude is a choice: it's available to you every moment, and as soon as you thank life you are flooded with a feeling of being blessed.

Why not take a moment right now and, if you are somewhere private, just say *out loud* what you are thankful for? . . . Right now . . . this very moment . . . for example, 'I'm thankful for the time to be able to be with myself.' Or, 'I'm thankful for the innate wisdom I'm uncovering. I'm thankful for the universe's grace in my life. I'm thankful to have the abundance to allow me to purchase a book such as this' . . . on and on. Just spend five minutes and share out loud, as if speaking to life. What are *you* most grateful for?

If your heart is open, and your gratitude genuine, you will be resting in an ocean of fullness, humility and grace.

Give it a whirl. Put the book down for a moment and just experience how graced you feel when you genuinely thank life. Gratitude is its own reward. When you consciously choose thankfulness you immediately feel flooded with blessedness.

✲ ✲ ✲

Australia is one of my favourite countries because, as a population, Australians seem to live with a natural attitude of gratitude. Just recently at lunch my partner Kevin and I were sitting in a small beachside café in Byron Bay when a large frilled lizard walked over to us, ostensibly begging for food. The people around us smiled fondly, as this was a common occurrence, and went back to their lunchtime conversation. The lizard came right up to my feet and, being from the States and completely unused to seeing such a beautiful reptile close up, I indulged myself in taking some moments to admire it; to take in its colourful striations, its thorny head, its bright beady eyes and its scaly skin. I was thoroughly delighted by its friendliness and ease around people. The couple on the table next to ours noticed my fascination and a warm conversation opened between us.

I explained how, though I spend half the year on the road in the southern hemisphere and am quite familiar with Australia, I'm still filled with wonder at its myriad delightful creatures. Being a New Yorker, I still feel gob-smacked by its variety of unique wildlife, and I'm as fascinated as a small child by it. The woman explained that she was a local, but worked full time in Brisbane, about a two-and-a-half hour drive away. She was a single mum and, though it was a long drive, she had really come to appreciate her home town in a way she'd never done before. She expressed how delighted she was to have a job in information technology, which was her specialty area and not one for which there was much demand in a small place like Byron Bay. She shared how her seven-year-old son got a chance to spend more time with his grandparents, and how much he loved that and, as she worked long hours, how grateful she was that her parents lived close by and were able to care for him.

By the end of the conversation I felt so full, so blessed by her refreshing view of life. Her attitude of gratitude was genuine, not some forced goody-two-shoes talk, but humble, straightforward gratitude, simply expressed. When she left the café, I turned to Kevin and said, 'What was it about that conversation that was so remarkably inspiring?'

'Gratitude,' he said. 'Many single mothers would have been complaining about the long drive, griping about the long working hours, and sad to have to let their son spend so much time with his grandparents. But she felt genuinely blessed in all ways. She was totally grateful for her life.'

This was clearly a woman who saw all life through the eyes of gratitude. For her, life was graced indeed.

Gratitude is a choice.

It is something you can live in and live *from* every day. And the moment you open your heart to how lucky, blessed and graced you are, grace begins to shower you!

I recently had an experience of this in such a powerful way that it blew me wide open.

I was giving a silent retreat, called *Falling into Grace*, at a beautiful spiritual centre set in glorious rolling green countryside. Throughout the weekend we had been clearing out veils, concepts and limitations, and opening ourselves into the boundless presence of grace that suffuses all our lives.

On the final morning, just as we were getting ready to go outside for a delicious al fresco celebration lunch, I asked the group if they would be willing to take a few moments to honour the staff who worked at the retreat centre. I explained that, though The Journey as a seminar company paid for the use of the premises, this money went to the non-profit foundation that ran the centre, and that the people who had served us with meals throughout the weekend had done so in selfless service, and were paid very modestly as they were really volunteers. They were serving truth, and we had all been blessed by their generosity and kindness. For a moment there was a hush in the hall as everyone took that in.

We had been served by fellow lovers of truth: their love and stillness permeated the food that they prepared for us and saturated the atmosphere of the entire centre, and I felt a heart pull to thank them and offer them small gifts to express our gratitude. Everyone agreed they'd like to take the extra time out and truly thank them with all our hearts.

I invited the staff on stage and to each, one by one, I began to express our gratitude. As I looked at their radiant, humble, shining faces and realised the immense offering they all had made in caring for us with so much love throughout the weekend, I became overwhelmed. Somehow, the gratitude I felt was too great to hold, and I burst into tears. I found myself bowing in deep namasté to each, with my hands over my heart in prayer position. I couldn't seem to bow low enough, or say words that could truly express our thanks. Finally, I found my head on the ground, and could only manage to stammer out, 'How can we ever thank you enough for your love of truth, your stillness, your humility, your generosity? These gifts cannot begin to express the thankfulness in our hearts.'

With each one I fell apart: we all did. And by the time it was over, and we had sung them the song 'Magnificence', the whole room was sobbing a flood of tears.

Our hearts were blown wide open. Spontaneously, everyone began to silently namasté each other in a huge outpouring of thanks.

At lunch it was as if we were sitting in an ocean of love, our hearts wide open, hushed humility everywhere. Midway through the meal, Kevin clinked his glass to speak, and asked if everyone would join us around the head table. He shared how recently, at the end of Accreditation Week in the UK, we had held an auction to raise funds for The Journey Outreach programme in South Africa.

In South Africa we have a beautiful, free-of-charge outreach programme, where our therapist volunteers go into schools, prisons, tribal communities, addict centres, AIDS orphanages, and youth groups, and offer Journeywork to all those children and adults who could otherwise never afford this kind of healing work and teaching. Everyone at our retreat already knew that I also offer The Journey Intensive weekend free to humanitarian-based organisations in South Africa, and that we go into the townships to serve in the underprivileged communities, and to train local people in the work.

Recently, Kevin explained, our Outreach organisation had been gifted a parcel of land, so that we could eventually build a classroom for the youngsters and a seminar hall for the adults, as well as individual offices and therapy rooms. This centre would be a completely free of charge sanctuary, open to all people – of any race, religion or background.

South Africa is a nation thirsty for healing, forgiveness and reconciliation, and we are already involved, with the government's blessing, in training many schoolteachers in Journeywork. And volunteers were pouring in to support our proposed centre. An architect had agreed to donate his time for the drawings; a solicitor had offered his services gratis, and we had even received some donations of bricks and cement. All we now needed were the funds to cover the main building materials and construction costs, and we estimated at that time for this very modest building we only needed around 30,000 Australian dollars. Kev was sharing that we were delighted to have raised the equivalent of over $3,000 in the UK, so we only needed $27,000 more to reach our goal. He said he hoped we might be able to raise some more to add to the pot, and that we'd decided to offer for auction a small personal item of mine; one of no significant monetary value.

Everyone's heart was already sweetly open, and we were all aware of how much the South Africans needed this help, how many lives would be transformed, how many souls would be touched.

Kevin started the bidding at $100, and everyone breathed a sigh of relief when the opening bid was received. He raised it to $200, then $300, $500, $700 and then, when the bid reached $1000 everyone fell silent. I was so overwhelmed at people's generosity of heart, and everyone was moved.

Someone raised their hand and quietly said, $2000. Again, silence . . . $2500 . . . then someone else, $3000. I could feel my heart beginning to explode as another bid $4000. Again, it all went quiet. $5000 . . . Silence . . . $6000 . . . when it got to $7000 the dam inside me broke, and my heart exploded in overwhelming gratitude and love. South Africa's dream for herself was becoming a reality.

By now Kevin had tears in his eyes and didn't know if he had the courage to ask for a higher bid. Everyone was totally silent, tears were streaming . . .

A woman raised her hand, and almost in a whisper said, '$10,000.'

Suddenly, everyone became aware that the Journey Outreach Centre was no longer an idea – it was manifesting right before our eyes. At that moment, the gratitude burst wide open, and everyone wanted to give. Kevin said he would find a couple of other items to offer and everyone wanted to be part of the vision as, in one great outpouring of offers, large and small, a total of over $50,000 was pledged for the centre. The building was going to get built.

It had happened in a heartbeat. A few minutes spent in open gratitude, and a building for healing had manifested. This dream *had* to be realised. It was the will of grace, and we were all vehicles in service to South Africa's vision. Gratitude simply had to have an avenue in which to express itself.

You know what the curious thing was? We were all aware that this wasn't even *our* vision. We had simply helped South Africa realise her own vision for herself. And yet where we were finally left was in an ocean of gratitude. We were graced by simply being allowed to offer. We all felt impossibly blessed to have been part of this holy action. We were privileged to be allowed to particpate, and gratitude was the gift, in and of itself.

Since that time the gratitude continues to flourish and South Africa's vision for herself has expanded enormously. From the humble beginnings of needing only a small, modest building, a new prayer arose and we are currently involved in creating an entire community centre in the heart of Soweto – a massive township near Johannesburg. In this centre, 5- to 24-year-olds can come to experience regular Journeywork to liberate their potential. And additionally we will be offering other empowering tools and skills, including literacy classes, African culture courses in music, art and dance, computer technology programmes and even business classes that will teach the teens how to write a CV. Over time, we hope the entire community will look upon this centre as a real sanctuary for realising their full potential.

And all this because a small group of people had to find an avenue to express their gratitude.

Gratitude can make *anything* happen. It has the power to bring to fruition the most impossible-seeming visions. And it does so effortlessly, joyously and humbly.

Gratitude and grace: they go hand in hand as two inseparable lovers.

✲ ✲ ✲

In my personal life, not a day goes by without taking time to thank life for its bounty. It's not that Kevin and I have some hollow daily practice. It's just that our hearts feel so grateful, so graced; we feel so lucky, so privileged that we cannot help but express it to each other several times each day.

Recently, for the first time ever in my life and in my fiftieth year, we *bought* a house. It's a modest three-bedroom bungalow with a flat roof, uneven floors and a dated 1960s look. But every day when I wake up and walk into the living room my heart is flooded with gratitude. This humble cottage is perched high on a cliff top, overlooking the sea in a tiny village in Wales. The garden was lovingly tended by the previous owner, and has grown mature and glorious in that love. The property is surrounded by common land that gently slopes down to the top of the cliffs, with the roaring surf beyond. Sheep graze in the meadows and roam freely through the village, and the air is fresh and sweet. I can't believe my lucky stars. The view from our living room and garden is so spectacular it takes my breath away; the stillness is so full you could cut it with a knife. This New Yorker is lulled to sleep at night by the sounds of ewes calling to their young lambs and the lambs answering back to their mothers. I'm beginning to think this may be one of the sweetest sounds on earth. And I sleep deeply, contentedly, in the embrace of gratitude that I feel to have such a healing and inspiring place in which to rest between our many seminar events.

And do you know what? The expression of gratitude makes life so juicy, so redolent with flavour, so fulfilling that life only gets fuller, richer, more graced, more bountiful.

When you see life through the eyes of gratitude, all of life becomes awash with grace. Everything begins scintillating with it.

And gratitude loves you so much that every moment is an invitation to experience the blessedness of life.

Invitation – Gratitude

Are there areas of your life that you have been taking for granted? Has life been showering you with grace, while you've answered back that your cup is half empty? It's time to realise that your half-empty cup is actually overflowing.

Gratitude always draws grace to itself. They are inextricably linked, and when you choose to give thanks to life for all that you've been given, grace showers you in return. Grace cannot refuse a grateful heart. So, you might like to get a pen and some paper, or perhaps take out a journal.

Take a few moments to become still and let your awareness go to all the ways you've been blessed in life: how you're blessed to have a pen and paper; how you're graced to have people in your life who love you; how bountiful it is that you can afford to eat healthy, nourishing food. Just let your mind rest in the huge magnificence of grace that has manifested in your life.

When you feel that your cup is overflowing, take your pen and begin letting that gratitude express itself on a page: keep asking yourself, 'What am I most grateful for?' Let all the small things come up, as well as the big ones. Remember the beauty of nature, and include your own wardrobe and the food you eat. Just let gratitude pour itself onto the page, and keep writing until several pages are full and you have emptied it all out.

Then just rest, bask, soak in the humility of realising just how lucky you are: regardless of your life's circumstances, grace is always present. Just rest in the open vastness that is experienced when the heart has been allowed to fully express its gratitude.

Gratitude begets more gratitude. Your list will likely become an endless outpouring. You might even like to make a daily practice of taking time to count your blessings, and put them onto paper for an entire week.

Once you start you may never want to stop, for gratitude is such a juicy experience. And the good news is it's a choice that is available to you in each and every moment.

love

'. . . and the greatest of these is Love.'

The way of love is not a subtle argument
The door there is devastation
Birds make great sky circles of their freedom
How do they do it?
They fall
And falling
They are given wings.

Rumi

It is true that the way of love is *not* a subtle argument. There has to be a willingness to allow the heart to be broken open a thousand times, and a thousand times more, for the vastness of love demands *all* of you. We cannot hold *anything* back from love: there must be a willingness to offer all of ourselves into the fire – even if it breaks our hearts; even if we are devastated by the power and immensity of its beauty, there must be the willingness to allow love to ravage us. For it is in the offering of our complete selves into this love that we fall, and in the falling that we are given wings and are free to soar on the wings of grace in the embrace of love.

There can be no half measures when it comes to love. Either you fall in completely or you flounder endlessly, grasping for something just out of your reach, and you taste only a small fraction of its immensity. Love simply requires all of you. And when you hold back any part of yourself from this ocean of love you end up denying yourself the joyous blessing of plunging into the infinite and swimming in grace.

It is not like you can say to love, 'Oh, I'll give *this* much of myself, but no more,' for the part you hold back will have a life of its own . . . it will fester and keep you feeling separate from the vast ocean of the infinite, constantly craving for it in its entirety. There is a beautiful song by Kirtana, some of the words of which express this realisation so poetically, so poignantly:

> . . . My beloved's love
> is like an ocean that will draw you in
> You can sink or swim –
> but I suggest you drown
> And come without your clothes *(in complete exposure)*
> She always knows when you've got clothes or fins
> And if you come up for air
> She's sure to spot you there
> And pull you down
>
> . . . She's so demanding
> let it be said she'll ask for everything
> And that little bit that's left
> To which you cling –
> She's gonna want that too . . .

Like Kirtana, I suggest you drown – for the only route into love is to surrender completely, even if your emotional dam breaks. There must be the willingness to offer yourself utterly so that all parts of you are totally exposed, including your so-called shadow parts that you are not so proud of. There must be a willingness to expose even the parts of you that are scared, greedy, wanting, insecure, unworthy, angry, frightened, needy, jealous, raging – grace is going to want *all* of you in your entirety, good, bad and indifferent. To experience real love is to offer every last bit of resistance up to it. In the willingness to expose all of yourself to love, all of grace floods in, surrounding, suffusing, permeating you.

Gurumayi says, 'That which you offer turns to gold. That which you hold back turns to coal.' The parts we hold back from grace wither and die away: sequestered from the light, no life can permeate them.

Love requires absolutely everything.

For many of us, even contemplating opening up and allowing all parts of ourselves to be exposed to love is a terrifying prospect. Often, we haven't even exposed the truth of our pain to *ourselves*, let alone offered it up to the dazzling, magnifying light of love. And yet, your very retreat from exposure is a retreat from love.

Love and exposure go hand in hand. You cannot have one without the other. Yet in the exposure of everything, all love is experienced to be surrounding, embracing and infusing everything that is brought into its light.

Last night, we held an informal satsang at our home for a few of our personal Journey friends and fellow lovers of truth. At it, one soft, radiant 40-year-old friend of mine was sharing how much she was missing her mother, who had just left on a plane for England after a particularly beautiful, rich and heart-opening six-week visit. Tears welled in her eyes as she openly shared her love for her mum, and her voice began to break as she sweetly exposed her vulnerability to the rest of us.

There was a hushed silence – we all felt gifted and opened by her tender exposure and the depth of love she feels for her mother. 'I just miss her so much . . .' her voice cracked; – her sentence trailed off as hot tears silently rolled down her cheeks.

I paused before I spoke, then quietly shared how awed I was by their closeness, by the depth of their love; and I admitted that many of us wished we felt that kind of heart-breaking love in our relationships with our mothers. I told her that this kind of love is very rare, and the fact that she was willing to have her heart broken would create a never-ending invitation to keep opening deeper in the love. For this love by nature is heart wrenching. And even as the heart breaks wide open, if you let go into it totally, it is discovered that it is love opening the gates wider into itself, exposing more of itself.

I told her how lucky she is to be able to feel love so fully, so humanly – for true love is like this: it wants all of you, and breaks you wide open.

There are so many people who, in feeling the immensity of love's power, resist its force and close a part of themselves off, as if to protect themselves from its intensity. But when they shut down to love, separation from life begins and a dull numbness can result: numbness to emotions, numbness to all of life, and an inability to find one's way back into love.

I was glad this was not the case with this radiant woman. She was open to love, and was right in the centre of its heartbreaking pain. I suggested that all she could do was ask for *more* heartbreak, to turn it up, open her entire being wider into it – for truly, the only way out of the pain is to go deeper into it. You have to be willing to say 'yes' to heartbreak, to surrender totally and pray for more. For as you let go completely into it, with no holding back, *your heartbreak is realised to be love itself.* And like a river held back by a dam, when you let the dam break, the falling in is experienced as a rush of ecstasy as Self merges into Self.

When she had finished opening into the immensity of the heart-break, her whole body relaxed and she looked totally relieved and at ease – she was left *as* love. So, instead of missing it, wishing for it, pining for a personal mother/daughter love, she had opened into the full force of her emotion, and was left as an ocean of love that was so large it was able to hold her relationship in its vaster context. She'd let the dam break and had opened into the infinite embrace of love itself.

I said it would be a gift if we all experienced this heartbreaking love, for it is the very nature of love to break through all our barriers of resistance and open us into an ocean vaster than could ever be imagined.

Our normally quietly disposed sound engineer began to turn red in the face as some sort of energy was building in his body. 'I never knew that love was this immense,' he blurted out, 'I've always held myself back from experiencing it, because it seemed too large to hold . . . I thought I would get hurt . . . that somehow it was bad to feel this intensity of feeling. I hadn't realised that love can be so heartbreaking, and I've held my love back from each of you in this room because I've felt afraid of its force.'

Then his voice cracked, his face turned bright red and something exploded inside. Floods of tears poured as he sobbed out, 'It's just so huge . . . this love . . . I never knew I'm so big . . . I've been playing at keeping myself so small . . . I was just afraid of the heartbreak . . . I never knew it was so huge . . . it really *is* a heartbreaking love.' Tears streamed down his cheeks, and he added, 'I feel so much gratitude for this love.'

To experience true love there has to be a willingness to have your heart broken by it a thousand times, for it is in the letting go into its force that the heartbreak itself is experienced as love. Then love is realised to be not a personal love, but an omnipresent field of love that permeates all of life. Its embrace is never ending, infinite and complete. And in this love you rest as total completion, utter peace, soaring freedom.

You are love itself.

The time has come to surrender completely. There is no escaping love – for it is *everywhere.*

✲ ✲ ✲

There is another requirement love has; not only does it want all of you in complete surrender, but it shows up when you expose everything to your*self*. When you are willing to shine the light of love onto the parts of yourself that you are not proud of – onto the unaccepted parts, the unloved parts, the unwanted emotions; when you shine the light of love into all the darkened corners of your soul, including the hidden, unwelcomed corners, love will begin to suffuse them, embrace them, permeate them – until you are left as nothing but love itself.

These parts of ourselves, like shy, unwanted children deserve to be welcomed into the light. They need it in order to experience true freedom.

So, to experience infinite love there must first be *self*-love, and that means welcoming every part of yourself into the open, into *total* acceptance. It's when we welcome these frightened children out into the open and accept what is here, that all healing can commence, in every aspect of our lives.

To heal, you must be willing to expose your true feelings in their entirety to the all-accepting light of love. Everything is welcome in love. Love is not picky or choosy, it loves absolutely everything.

On the final morning of a recent retreat, Alistair, a beautiful, radiant man from New Zealand, stood on stage to celebrate his fiftieth birthday by opening himself to the fullness of the love in the room. I had instructed everyone to share openly with him what qualities they saw in him, and asked him to open and receive their praise.

People began to call out what they saw, 'I see strength,' 'I see vulnerability,' 'I see tenderness,' 'I see wisdom.' They shouted from various corners of the room, 'I see intensity,' 'kindness,' 'laser-like intelligence,' 'peace,' the list went on and on.

Sitting next to him on the stage, I could sense that it was beginning to be too much for him to hold: it was like he was subtly bracing himself, not allowing the words to fully penetrate; as if he couldn't quite allow in all the beauty that was being reflected back to him. His body, though open, was also a bit stiffened; as if he was afraid he might lose control or break if he really allowed the truth to reach inside him.

Quietly, I whispered, 'I suggest you drown. You can't hold back this tidal wave with some imagined shield. I suggest you surrender . . . just drown in the love.' And something broke – a chink cracked open and, in one moment, all armour crumbled and fell away. Tears started streaming.

With no barriers there, the room became an ocean of love – unbridled, unguarded love. He was sitting there for all to see in complete unguarded exposure, and everyone was welcome to reflect back to him what was truly there.

'Ocean of love,' someone said. 'Innocence,' said another. 'All love,' I said quietly, 'All love.'

And so it is: all love is here the moment complete and total exposure happens.

Recognising the power that exposure has in opening us into the ocean of love, I asked everyone if they'd like to experience it for themselves, and they paired up throughout the room, sitting facing each other.

I suggested that everyone take off their imaginary armour, and just be willing to open into complete exposure. I had each partner begin by saying, 'Thank you for your openness. I'm sure I have the same issues as you. You are my mirror, and it's such a privilege to sit here with you. Thank you for exposing *my* issues through your openness.'

I then suggested that they simply ask their partner, 'What feelings have you been hiding from in yourself? These shy, hidden emotions that you haven't wanted to expose, even to yourself . . . if there was something that you hadn't admitted, something secret that you wished wasn't there, I wonder what that might be? What are some of the secret fears that you are not proud of? What have you not even admitted to yourself, let alone shared with someone else? What have you never spoken out loud before?'

Everyone was instructed to ask these questions with great love and compassion, really welcoming complete exposure of the hidden bits, the frightened parts, and when their partner openly responded they were to answer, 'I forgive you . . . the universe forgives you. As part of everything that is, all forgiveness is here.'

Then they had to ask again, 'What else are you ashamed of? What else have you been afraid to admit, even to yourself?'

Once again, the partner responded fully, and again they replied with words of forgiveness, 'I forgive you . . . All of life forgives you.'

They continued in this way until the partner was *completely* emptied out, washed clean and all was forgiven.

Then the partners switched roles and did the same thing . . . emptying out all the shy bits, the parts they were ashamed of, the emotions they had never allowed themselves to feel and the behaviours they had never been proud of. Once again, they too were offered complete forgiveness, universal forgiveness and utter acceptance.

The room felt awash with love. It was like all the holding back had been cleared out and all that remained was love itself. We all felt it.

In the offering up to love of all the unloved bits we were left as *all* love, all acceptance . . . total peace.

Anything you hold back creates separation. Anything you offer up to grace gets transmuted into love.

Self-love leads you into the ocean of love. The river flows into the sea, and all the dead twigs it carried dissolve and become part of the ocean.

Invitation – Love

So, why don't you give it a go? Find out for yourself the power of exposure and acceptance. If you have someone in your life you feel you could openly and honestly share the above process with, this would probably be the most exposing way to experience this lesson. But if you don't, you can do it privately, on your own.

If you are doing it alone I recommend that you take at least fifteen to twenty minutes completely by yourself in a private and quiet place. You can even put on the companion CD. You can begin by taking some deep breaths in and letting them out . . . allowing your awareness to rest on the breath, as your breathing slows down and your being settles.

Once you feel still, settled and open you can imagine that you are taking some imaginary armour off; armour that has in the past stopped you from getting access to the full intensity of your emotions. So, imagine doing that right now.

Then make a sincere prayer, or put out a genuine intention to the universe that you are willing with all your heart to expose yourself to all the unwanted bits, the emotions you've been ashamed to admit you have, the secret fears, the things you've done that you're not proud of.

And then open your heart . . . make your heart as wide as the world – wide enough to include all these shy parts, and the timid, undeserving parts – and put out a welcome to them. Just welcome up the emotions, the words, the secrets, and speak them out into the room. Finally let them have expression; let the totality of them be admitted, seen, heard and released.

You can begin with words like, 'What I'm not proud of is . . .' or 'I've never been willing to admit that I feel . . .' or 'I've always secretly felt . . .' or 'I never wanted anyone to know this, but . . .'

After each full emptying out, say the words, 'I forgive myself. All forgiveness is here. Life forgives me.'

Continue emptying out and forgiving in just this way until you feel wide open, washed clean, and at peace. You can let this take as long as it needs. The important part is to *voice* these things out *loud*. You need to get them up and out. Of course, at first it may seem a bit awkward to be talking to a room, but you'll eventually feel how liberating it is to finally express the inexpressible, to allow up the unacceptable and to free the hidden secrets. It's in speaking it out loud that there is a genuine release.

Then make certain that you always follow each emptying out with forgiveness: your self-forgiveness, God's forgiveness, life's forgiveness. At the end, you will feel as if your heart is wide open and you are resting in an ocean of love.

Love and exposure: these are two friends that go hand in hand.

✲ ✲ ✲

Love is an embrace that is so vast, so infinite that it not only suffuses all aspects of your*self* but it permeates all of life itself. It is a limitless embrace that is the very fabric of the universe, and it cannot be subdivided into human-sized portions, for it is everywhere. Love is so huge it contains all of life.

So often we make the mistake of believing that the love we experience is attributable to one special person. In our hearts we mistakenly believe that this person is responsible for the love we are feeling and, instead of remaining wide open in the vaster embrace of the infinite, we contract our awareness down to that one person and then project our narrow band of love their way, personalising the love, believing that the object of our affection is responsible for creating the feelings of in-loved-ness we are experiencing in that moment.

When we do this we create separation, projection and *need*, for if someone else is responsible for our feeling these blissful sensations then without that person we are bereft, lost and incomplete. So need arises and soon we begin to mistake *need* for love, believing that it is natural to need someone, indeed believing that the essential nature of love is need.

This colossal mistake creates much of the suffering in our lives. It's like we build a sandcastle of our love, invest all of our energy, life force, and attention, directing all our loving thoughts towards this one imaginary object. But, as with all sandcastles no matter how well we construct them, in time someone inevitably tramples over them and ruins them, or the tide simply comes in and washes them away.

If you are truthful with yourself you will realise that objectified love is merely a self-created, idealised illusion that you constructed so that you could indulge in a little fantasy, fun and make-believe. But ultimately, in the light of day, it is all seen to be no more than a beautiful sand creation that gave you pleasure for a short time while you gave yourself permission to believe in it.

Believing that your love and happiness depend on someone else 'out there' is like believing your joy comes from the sandcastle you built on the beach. The sandcastle is an *expression of* your joy, not the *cause* of it. And the sandcastle and your projected, objectified love have as much reality, substance and durability as each other.

No one on the outside can create your love. Love simply *is*. And it is experienced when you open your whole being to it and expose yourself to the beauty of all of life.

Certainly, others are a reflection of this love, for they too are permeated with it. It's why, when you look at a young kitten, or a newborn baby, or a freshly bloomed crocus on the first day of spring, love arises. It's not that those things *caused* you to experience love, it's just that in your openness you recognised it, and love spontaneously washed through your consciousness.

So often, what happens is that we feel open, humbled or awed by someone or something we see in life and immediately, in our desire to capture the moment, to somehow hold onto it, we look outside ourselves to find who was responsible for its arising. Immediately, the one we lay eyes upon becomes the cherished one, and we pray that in their presence the same feelings of exhilaration and bliss will come bubbling up from within again. It's like Cupid's arrow has pierced our heart and the first object we see we begin to dote on and crave. With this initial mistake, we begin to long to be with the 'loved one', to spend more time in their presence, hoping to get the 'hit' again. And if the 'fix' isn't immediately apparent we feel somehow lost, separated, bereft. It hadn't given us the longed for result; it didn't satiate us and our thirst was not slaked.

But, instead of recognising that the other person can't be responsible for the way we feel, that it was just a mistake to begin with, we turn up our expectations. The longing gets sharper and the need for love grows more intense. We try to duplicate it, recreate it, capture it, make it happen again. And because we've collapsed our awareness and thereby lost sight of the vaster embrace of infinite love, we begin to feel empty, alone, needy. So, no matter how long we are in this other person's presence, we somehow *still* feel alone, separated. We crave an all-embracing love, but we get locked into becoming an addict, a junkie: wanting, lusting, obsessing, waiting for our next fix, even though some deeper inner knowing knows it will never be enough to complete us.

Very often, in collapsing our love and projecting it onto one person in this way, we feel separated from God and, feeling alone and forsaken, of course we look to more and more people 'out there' to fill this empty need inside.

Our neediness then becomes a force that repels the other person. For how could anyone else fill up the empty hole inside us? How could anyone else shoulder the huge responsibilities of being the catalyst for, and the impetus behind, our experience of love? Then we end up disillusioned, blaming and resentful.

The time has come to stop believing in your fairytale romance. It's time to crush your illusory sandcastles. It's time to stop pretending you don't know who you are.

No one else can make you complete. Nor can they give you the love you crave. For love can neither be given nor received. It is an ocean that can be experienced. It is an infinite embrace that you can joyously dance in with someone else, but ultimately no one can give it to you.

Sometimes in marriage people refer to their partner as 'my other half'. Whenever I hear that I cringe; for how can someone else complete you? And does it also imply that they are only half a person? Such a burden is placed on the other if they feel that they are responsible for filling your needs. Your neediness has nothing to do with them – you just lost sight of the infinite and in that constant feeling of being separate from God, you spend your life seeking out someone to make you whole again. Indeed, your neediness can end up *repelling* the person you so desire.

In the past, when I offered couples counselling, I would so often come across one or other partner being repelled by the neediness and dependency of the other. They would confide in me, 'No matter how much I say I love them, no matter how much I show them affection or spend time caring, it's like it's never enough. Nothing is ever going to fill their empty hole inside. It's a bottomless pit.'

One man complained that he felt like he was just some inanimate object, used simply to fill the emptiness in his wife. She thought she was being attentive and loving towards him, but what he felt was her neediness drawing on him, not her love coming his way. He experienced her as having an unslakeable craving for attention that he felt ill equipped to fulfil. He admitted that, ultimately, her neediness was a turn off – that her trying to glean her sense of self, her feeling of wholeness from him, was actually pushing him away and jeopardising their marriage. He said, 'It's such a shame, because I really do love her – I always have, but her neediness is driving us apart.'

His wife had so objectified her husband, become so dependent on him for her sense of wholeness and indeed for love itself, that he was repulsed by it. It was literally driving him away.

Neediness is a repelling force that has nothing to do with love.

Are there relationships in your life that are based more on need than on love? Right now, just bring your awareness to a particularly important relationship in your life. Check your body. Be real with yourself. Are there ways in which you secretly, or even openly feel that this person *gives* you the feeling of love? Or do you believe you *give* them theirs?

What if there were some huge imaginary energetic umbilical cord tying you unhealthily and co-dependently to this person? And what if you were to try an experiment right now?

Imagine that there might be such an energetic tie connecting the two of you. And imagine that a loving angel is going to take some divine scissors and cut that tie. Now imagine that when this cord is severed, a huge all embracing love channels back through it and suffuses and embraces your loved one. Then imagine that this same infinite, all-embracing love comes flooding down your half of the cord, and that you are suddenly suffused with and embraced by this love.

What if, instead of being collapsed into and co-dependent on each other's love, you danced lightly together in an infinite field of love? Fully complete in your realisation of it, and graced by being able to have a partner to flow through life with you.

What if you just delighted in your partner's presence, and felt blessed by not being needed? What if you felt completely, utterly free, embraced by love, and lucky to share life with your partner, all the while fully acknowledging they *can't give you anything* other than to point you deeper into your own experience of love?

And what if you required *nothing* of this other person? And what if they required *nothing* of you? Instead, what if in all freedom you chose to dance the dance of life together – blessed in the joy of each other's good company, privileged to be allowed to have a partner to celebrate life with in the embrace of love.

What if the embrace was so completely complete that, if that partner was taken away by life's circumstances, your wholeness was discovered to be no less whole, the vastness no less vast, the completeness no less complete. And what if, in all relationships in life, you held all people in this lighter, vaster context? I wonder how joyous and blessed your relationships might become.

What if *all of life* appeared in this freer, lighter embrace?

✲ ✲ ✲

I remember one lazy summer's afternoon when I was about twelve years old, my grandmother, who had a Master's degree in philosophy and religion, drew me into her little breakfast nook to share some jasmine tea and have a philosophical chat about the nature of love. I always felt graced with Grandma's wisdom, and hung on her every word. I adored her with all my heart, the way young children do, and I listened to each word, eager for it to somehow penetrate deeply, so that I could hold onto her pearls of wisdom for the rest of my life.

She confided in me that when she was newly married, Grandpa had been fiercely jealous if she even so much as looked at another man. Her eyes twinkled in ironic remembrance of those times: she had been quite a radical woman for an American in the late 1920s. To begin with, women weren't supposed to go to university at that time, let alone do postgraduate work. She'd been a suffragette, fighting for women's rights and she recollected how she'd dressed in the risqué styles of the flappers, and shared how she'd dared to go without a bra. The fact that hemlines were so short for those days was already quite a rebellious statement for a young woman, but she took it to the limit and actually bandaged her chest to make it look mashed and fashionably flat.

'To your traditionally brought up grandfather, I must have seemed a real libertine,' she chuckled to me, as she saw through the innocence of her own then-perceived recklessness. 'It's not like we were wanton. We had plans to become missionaries in China, and we both had very strong spiritual beliefs, but of course we had to wait for Grandpa to get his PhD and by then, war was brewing and we were unable to follow our calling. We had been married over two years when the jealousy issue came to a head, and you know how much I adore your grandfather – I only have eyes for him.' I knew this was true, for the pair seemed like two lovebirds, still madly, deeply in love even in their eighties.

'Well,' she continued, 'Grandpa used to fly into jealous rages, making scenes if I even had a conversation with one of my friends' husbands. One night we were all at a dance together and politely my friend's husband filled in one of the slots on my dance card. Well, Grandpa lost it. He packed me up in the Model T and drove me home in an enraged silence and, as soon as we came through the front door, he exploded.

'The next day, I sat him down and told him that if he ever treated me in that way again I would leave him. Now, you know my dear, that would have broken my heart, but I wasn't willing to be suffocated by his jealousy. Jealousy and love have nothing to do with each other.

'Grandpa admitted to me that he was just a humble son of a farmer who had grown up as one of twelve brothers, and when he met me he thought I was the most beautiful sight he had ever seen. He couldn't believe his lucky stars that this hick from the backwoods of

Nebraska could possibly be attractive to someone as lovely as me. And, he thought if he felt this way, surely *all* other men must suffer in silence as they looked at me!'

Grandma admitted she was deeply moved by Grandpa's adoration of her, and she laughed at the silliness of his jealousy, 'It's not like I'm some stunning beauty, my dear. It's just that he was seeing me through the rose-coloured filter of love. We were both madly in love with each other – it was love at first sight.

'But as much as I love your grandpa, and I love him so much that it still makes my heart skip, I won't be smothered by it, trapped by it or made less in it – because that's not love; that is need, my dear, and there's a huge difference between love and need.'

Innocently, I asked Grandma, 'Well, how did you end up staying together? Did Grandpa stop getting jealous?'

She paused, and said, 'Well, yes dear . . . love demanded it. I insisted that his love for me be so great that he face his jealousy down and finish with it – that those were the only conditions upon which I would stay in the relationship. And he knew I meant it.

'I explained to Grandpa my philosophy on love . . . that you must love freely, with an open heart and an open hand. You must treat love as if it is a delicate bird that comes to delight you by sitting in the palm of your hand. You cannot close your fist, for you will smother and kill it with too tight a grasp.

'No, simply, love demands trust. You must set your bird free to soar, and if it doesn't come back, it was never yours. But if it returns to you, for as long as your hand remains open it is yours forever. So, my dear, when you fall in love with your first beloved remember to love with an open hand.'

I've remembered my grandmother's words from that day on, but now I might change the ending to, 'If the bird returns to you, then you are blessed by it for yet one more day – for nothing belongs to us, nothing is owned by us.' Love is free to soar on the wings of freedom with no strings attached.

You can't own love. You can only bask in it, rest in it, be graced and blessed in it. And in it people will come and go.

I remember so clearly at the end of my twenty-year former marriage that I was absolutely aware, right through the entire leave-taking process, that there was an essential love that was utterly untouched by any of it. The embrace remained whole, complete and free with both the coming and the going of that deeply devoted relationship.

So, how do you love completely and still stay wide open in an ocean of love, dancing freely in its embrace with your partner? I can't say that I've got it completely figured out, but I do know that I've fallen so deeply in love with this infinite embrace that I am not willing to contract into some narrow, tight idea of love just for one soul. I experience love as an all-embracing ocean.

I remember in meeting my new partner and lover, Kevin, that I felt scared. I didn't want to sacrifice this omnipresent ocean of love for an ephemeral love that might come and go. I'm sure I must have seemed somewhat elusive, even fickle, in the early days of our relationship. In our intimate conversations I often spoke only of my love of truth, and I didn't bring personal, objectified love into it.

When I first realised I was beginning to sense the delicate whispers of attraction I immediately became hyper-vigilant: I didn't want anyone waltzing into my life and surreptitiously stealing this realisation of universal love.

I feared that personal love would somehow take me away from the vast embrace of divine love. But these were just unfounded fears born from my past concepts about what love is. Because nothing can steal *this* love from you: *this* love is who you are, and it is shining in everything.

I recall that early on in our relationship I kept Kevin at arm's length as we carried on a long-distance love affair thousands of miles apart, with me in California and Kev in the UK. In this way I was 'safe' and could make certain that my love for a man would in no way interfere with my greater love of truth.

I already knew which love I could count on, as this ocean of love is the only love that is eternal, infinite. People come and go in our lives, but *this* love is endless. So I approached the relationship softly, checking the waters to see if romantic love in any way obscured my experience of the vaster embrace. At first, it was only a toe-dip. Then, weeks later, ankle deep . . . months later, knee deep. And a whole year later, I took the full plunge.

Through the course of that year I learned that I could feel all kinds of powerful emotions and sensations: feelings of overwhelming attraction, chemicals of bliss in the body as a rush of arousal would wash through; deep appreciation or the feeling of being incredibly blessed would arise from nowhere and then sensitivity and shyness might surprise me; a thrill of excitement, like an out-of-control train, might completely take me over. The whole emotional panoply of romantic love came to dance through consciousness, but the vaster embrace remained completely untouched. Consciousness delighted in the myriad ecstatic, trying, devastating, blissful, beautiful, soaring emotions that came through it. And still the sky remained whole, complete no matter how big a storm came flooding across it.

Over the first year of our courtship I was the most truly human I've ever been, feeling raw, unguarded emotions without any protection – and through it all I remained identified with the vaster context in which everything was happening.

I survived. And I passed the test. It was safe to love: to love wholeheartedly, with abandon, rambunctiously, totally and turbulently. And I discovered that this 'I', the essential love that I am, remained whole throughout it all.

To this day, Kevin and I dance together lightly and deeply in this love. There is deep appreciation, daily gratitude; there are misunderstandings, out and out arguments; there is ecstasy, sublime lovemaking, out-of-control passion, gentleness, kindness, deep caring, huge mutual support – and ultimately it is all taking place in the vaster embrace of *this* love.

Though we both work for The Journey in service to truth, helping thousands worldwide to experience freedom and healing, *we face the same direction* – our joint focus is on freedom and service; our vision is the same, and we both feel immensely privileged to be allowed to dance in this embrace, partnering each other as the one love.

Our schedules often take us to different parts of the world for weeks on end, but the completeness remains completely complete as we keep our awareness on the vaster context. Our greatest love is the love of truth, and our relationship is a gift from grace that allows us to dance fully in the vaster embrace, whether physically together or apart. And love is still teaching us both: we still feel like beginners learning our first lessons.

When truth is number one in your life everything else falls into place behind it and in it; and all is graced by it. It seems that the deeper love opens into love, the more true and honest we must be with ourselves and with life. Love demands all exposure from us, and leaves us as an ocean of the infinite.

From time to time attachment does arise for me. After some time of being apart, some physical longing to be in the presence of my beloved mate still comes up for me. Then I take time to choose to let go of the strings of attachment, and to open wider into the embrace, for I do not want any form of need to come into our love and sully it.

And sometimes when we come back together shyness arises, and we have to open into a greater exposure and openly reveal our emotions to one another.

It's a constant learning, and the teaching is one that I'm sure I'll never fully get to the bottom of. For love is endless in its teaching, as well as in its embrace. And you should feel free to let yourself love deeply and well: just leave need and attachment out of the picture. No ownership can abide in true love, for love cannot be won, earned, owned or required. To love is to never fully know whether or not the other will be there in the next moment. To love is to surrender completely to this *moment*.

Love simply *is*.

Indeed, as Christ said, '. . . and the greatest of these is Love.' That's Love with a capital L . . . a love that never ends; a love so great that it is here before you are born, remains throughout your life, and will still be here long after the passing of your physical form.

This is a Love worth making a marriage with.

forgiveness

True forgiveness is one of the most healing, releasing and freeing gifts we give to ourselves.

A life full of open forgiveness is a life of grace.

True forgiveness is one of the most healing, releasing and freeing gifts we give to ourselves. A life full of open forgiveness is a life of grace.

When Gaby, one of the directors of The Journey Seminars, softly suggested that this book would not be complete without a chapter on forgiveness, she stopped me in my tracks. I looked at her and thought, 'Of course! It's so obvious. How could it be otherwise?' For forgiveness is the natural, outward expression of the open acceptance that is intrinsic to freedom. The two are inseparable. In all acceptance forgiveness arises, and when we forgive we are bathed in all acceptance. And peace is the final result – peace on all levels of being.

Personally, I feel an overwhelming gratitude to life for teaching me the immense healing power of forgiveness. For forgiveness was the catalyst for my own healing journey, and all of the Journeywork now being taught around the world was born from the willingness of an open heart to release the pain of the past and forgive unconditionally. In Journey seminars, no matter how many processes we do – no matter how diligently we face and clear issues; no matter how much hurt and pain is released or old stories of victim-ness exposed; no matter how many silent saboteurs are unearthed nor how many strategies of avoidance recognised; no matter how many games of the ego are penetrated – still, in the end, it all comes to wholeness and completion with the simple act of forgiveness. Because it is in forgiveness that true healing begins. Healing in a very real way – physically, cellularly, in our relationships, with life and most importantly with ourselves.

It could even be said that healing and forgiveness are synonymous.

I remember once reading in an enlightened master's book, 'The root cause of all illness is lack of forgiveness.' I would add to that, 'And the beginning of all healing starts with forgiveness,' for if we lived in open acceptance and all forgiveness each and every moment, we would welcome life as it is with open arms, with no resistance. It is only with resistance that friction and suppression begin, opening the eventual possibility of a whole host of physical symptoms.

Forgiveness is a route to freedom on all levels of being.

To get a taste of what I'm saying, just try an experiment right now. Think of an issue that you've not really come to terms with; something you're not proud to have done, or perhaps something you regret saying, or perhaps some opportunity that has passed you by, that you've never really forgiven yourself for not taking action on. Make it real. Find some mistake you made, something you blame yourself for, or some memory or aspect of your life that you've not forgiven yourself for, and for now surround it with a bath of acceptance . . . Take your time . . . Now say the words – *literally, say the words* – 'I forgive myself' . . . Say them internally again and this time, really mean it . . . 'I forgive myself' . . . Now open into what it really feels like to finally and deeply forgive yourself and say out loud, 'I forgive myself.'

Now check how you're feeling. When I just did that exercise I could feel some tears welling up behind my eyes, for the truth is I so needed to hear those words right now. And I felt a subtle release, a soft letting go into simplicity, into gratitude, into peace. What was your experience? Did you feel a gentle release or a soft letting go, and experience at least a brief moment of peace?

Forgiveness can be one of the simplest, truest acts of release we experience in life. It's so simple, yet so powerful. And the results of it reverberate not only through our own beings, but to all those concerned.

So much of Journeywork centres on forgiveness, and one thing I learned is, you can't fake it. You can't just repeat the words, paying lip service to the idea of forgiveness. It has to come from an open heart. It has to be real. Otherwise it is a pointless exercise that simply glosses over the issue. For, in truth, in order to forgive with all your heart, you must be willing to *open* your heart, and face and release the pain there.

Real forgiveness requires humility. And it is by nature a humbling experience. It means you have to give up your righteous indignation, get off the soapbox, and let go of the blame game and the pride of knowing you're right. It means you have to be willing to drop the whole victim story and finally soften your stance and, if necessary, let your heart be broken wide open. Then when the words 'I forgive you' are spoken there is a palpable presence of grace that floods in instantly behind them and you can tangibly feel the healing commence.

This was a lesson I learned personally many years ago when, through grace, I healed naturally from a very large tumour. During that time I had a knowing that part of my healing would lie in uncovering old cell memories that were part of the co-creation of the tumour. I knew that if somehow I could unearth the stored pain, and face and release the consciousness of it, somehow my body would go about its own process of healing. I had read reams of research on cellular healing and seen dozens of case studies, and one fact stood out above all the rest: when we suppress a strong emotion, or a trauma, or painful memory – when it gets stuffed down, or tucked away, or swept under the carpet – a measurable chemistry is released in the body, which can block certain cell receptors. This shut-down impairs the cells' natural ability to communicate with the other cells in the body and if, over time, that emotional issue, or 'cell memory,' remains stored in the cells and the cell receptors remain closed, then, in time, disease can occur in that part of the body.

I also knew that many of the people who had been successful at cellular healing (without drugs or surgery) had spontaneously gained access to these old memories, and when they released them the body went about its own natural process of healing.

There was no doubt I understood the scientific principles behind it, and had read all the books, and recognised the truth behind the research – *but no one had given us a method to access the cell memories and clear them*. And you can understand all the science on the planet and know all the statistics, but without a step-by-step process those case histories of spontaneous healing are nothing but a bunch of pretty words.

Well, I was about three weeks into my own healing journey and I was beginning to feel pretty damn sorry for myself. Obviously, I knew that part of my healing lay in uncovering these old cell memories, but I still didn't have a clue how to go about it – I didn't even know where to begin!

I'd tried everything that I knew of in the natural health field and I had to face the fact that I had not succeeded. Here it was, three weeks into my healing process, and the tumour was just as hard and just as large as ever.

I was getting a massage one particular day and I clearly remember the moment a chink appeared in my armour of arrogance. As I was lying there I reflected on my twenty years of experience and expertise in the alternative health field, and I had to admit, with all the knowledge I'd attained, still I'd failed. In fact, when I inwardly admitted the real truth, I felt myself to be a complete and abject failure. I didn't even know what questions to ask anymore or where to turn.

Then something inside cracked, and I suddenly realised I didn't really know *anything*. I fell into a helpless, hopeless despair. Internally, something finally just gave up.

I gave up. I surrendered, and in that surrender I felt myself fall into the soft embrace of innocence. I fell into the unknown. I didn't know *anything* anymore. In that simple admission something let go. I felt a palpable release. And spontaneously I opened into a bath of peace. I felt cradled in it and melted into it until there was no inside, no outside, just peace and a simple innocence everywhere. From this innocence I heard a humble prayer emerge, 'Please let me be guided to uncover what's stored inside this tumour.' As soon as it was spoken it was released into the unknown and I just lay there in the emptiness, not expecting anything, just being.

Then, suddenly and unexpectedly, I *was* guided, and when I uncovered the memory stored in the tumour, my arrogance instantly resurrected itself and loudly shouted in my head, 'It can't be that memory – you *know* all about that old memory of childhood violence. You've been through all that. You are *so* finished with it.' But I realised I couldn't afford to listen to my arrogant know-it-all mind talk, so I opened my being and decided to really welcome the memory, to genuinely face and release all the pain that came with it. But in spite of the fresh opening and release I still ended up in that same place of acceptance I'd been at for years.

I asked the peace in the room, 'Am I complete?' The response was simple and clear, '*No*.' Again I fell into despair. Here I'd uncovered a so called cell memory, but I didn't even know if it was the right one, and I'd already dealt with it in the past! I felt helpless, confused, totally at a loss. Once again, something inside me just gave up. And once again I fell into the soft innocence of not knowing anything, having no answers, not even knowing what to ask anymore.

I melted into the innocence, and as I did I heard another prayer give birth to itself, 'Please, somehow, let me be guided to completion – I don't know how to complete. I don't even know if this is the right memory and, even if it is, I've arrived at the same place of acceptance that I've been at for years. Please, show me how to complete.'

There was silence. I didn't expect an answer. Time rested. Then spontaneously, unexpectedly, out of the emptiness a single word emerged: 'Forgiveness.'

Now of course my arrogant thinking mind raised its mouthy head and said, 'Forgiveness? What a load of crap, Brandon, you've so long since accepted this whole issue; you've got it handled. You've done so much work on it – been there, done that, got the T-shirt on it. What difference can forgiveness make?'

But I thought, 'You know what, I can't afford to listen to my negative thoughts. Besides, I have nothing to lose by forgiving, and possibly everything to gain.' So I gave it my best shot.

And during the process of forgiveness that followed I realised *there is a quantum DIFFERENCE between acceptance and forgiveness.*

I had been at a place of acceptance for many years. That acceptance allowed me to carry my story of nobility around with me – how I'd been so-o-o noble, so-o-o compassionate, so-o-o understanding, that I'd come to accept the violence that had taken place. Kind, compassionate (arrogant!) Brandon.

And to forgive totally, unconditionally, I had to open my heart, get off my soapbox, give up thirty years of my blame game, and completely and wholeheartedly forgive.

It hurt, because I had to face down my pride. I had become so falsely noble, so saintly in my own eyes, and I had to own up to my own righteousness and finally give up the whole story – a story that had been a defining experience and expression of who I held myself to be. I had to give up my *attachment* to the story that I had been wronged by life. And when I finally forgave, when I truly opened my heart and completely forgave, the whole story of blame fell away and the consciousness connected with it was no more.

My story was over.

While I was forgiving, I realised that the tumour had never been clinging to me. *I'd* been clinging to it, and thirty years of dragging my victim story with me, finished in that one instant of pure, honest forgiveness.

The rest of the story is history and three and a half weeks later I was diagnosed to be completely tumour free – no drugs, no surgery.

The healing power of forgiveness is palpably strong. It can heal bodies. It can heal lives. It can heal relationships. It can even heal entire nations. And it truly is a *gift you give yourself.*

✡ ✡ ✡

So often we make the mistake of believing we are forgiving the other person for *their* sake, but the truth is, whenever you forgive you release the *consciousness* of the whole story that you've been previously holding onto and nursing, and when it's gone *you* are the one who is freed.

In my experience there are really three aspects to forgiving. Firstly, there has to be a willingness to let go of our attachment to our story, to admit to and let go of our arrogance. We have to be willing to drop our self-righteousness and give up the 'juiciness' we feel by being superior, right, on higher moral ground.

Next, we need to empty out. We need to get real and recognise that behind the arrogance is the real pain and hurt we feel, and we need to open our being and let all the raw feelings that had previously been suppressed and unexpressed be fully felt. We need to release all the pent-up emotion, the words and the consciousness that were hiding behind our pseudo-armour of false nobility and blame. All of the genuine pain needs to be released.

Then thirdly, once all the hurt has been met, expressed and let go of, our hearts are open to uncovering the true learning inherent in the situation. We are open to experiencing what the other has gone through, and we may realise they were probably doing the best they could at that time within the confines of their own past conditioning, dramas and pain. Once we've released our own pain, our heart feels a natural compassion and understanding of others' pain.

And it's from that understanding and compassion that real forgiveness arises. It arises naturally, almost unavoidably, and it is completely unconditional. Once you've emptied out fully, forgiveness floods in to fill the void as a natural expression of grace. Forgiveness releases you completely from your story of pain and allows you to move forward in freedom in your life.

Indeed, forgiveness can become a route to freedom, if you are willing to drop your arrogance, open and release the stored pain, and allow natural compassion for the others to arise.

In it all, humility is the key. For in true forgiveness, humility is always present.

✡ ✡ ✡

There is one very potent aspect of forgiveness that really needs highlighting here. Over the years of experiencing and witnessing thousands of Journey processes, I've realised that for true healing to occur one *must* empty out all the stored pain, hurt, blame, hatred. We cannot just by-pass the emptying out and releasing process and jump straight to genuine forgiveness, because the consciousness connected to the issues remains stored inside the body and it continues to have a life of it's own. And that can be damaging.

Very often, people who are new to Journeywork think they can trick grace. They naively believe they can avoid facing their own issues, by-pass feeling the true pain of past traumas, circumvent releasing the words and consciousness connected to them, and instead jump straight to forgiveness. They fool themselves into believing that healing will happen automatically once words of forgiveness have been spoken, and they believe they can just gloss over their own pain by being 'Mr nice guy' or 'Ms nice girl', by offering 'sincere' forgiveness.

I call this pseudo-forgiveness. It just doesn't work.

When I point out that they're just glossing over their own issues, and that once they've released the *real* hurt, the opportunity exists for *real* forgiveness to arise of its own accord, they will often counter with, 'But I don't want to say anything mean or hurtful. I realise that person is not here right now but I just don't want to put any bad thoughts out there.'

I always answer like this, 'The issue and its associated emotions are already stored inside your body. So, you could take forty-five minutes to humbly, honestly and completely admit, face and empty out all the stored pain, feel and release the unexpressed emotions, clear the entire issue and be finished with it for the rest of your life; or you can leak it out, hurting that person continually for the rest of their life.

'Those hateful, hurtful words are already present inside you. And you can finally admit them, release them and be done with them once and for all, or you can harbour these thoughts inside you and let their destructive work be ongoing, for I promise you the other person is already getting your strong non-verbal communication on a daily basis.

'And what do you think is more healing for you, facing and clearing it or holding onto it, stringing it out over time?'

Of course, they always admit that it's more healing to get real, open up and empty out the true pain, hurt and upset now. Yes, there may be some intense feelings to be felt and strong words that need to be voiced for a few moments, but that is far more healing than stuffing it back down and letting it leak out on a daily basis, eking out the underlying pain over the years.

For forgiveness to be truly effective and healing *you* must be free and you *must* be true.

✲ ✲ ✲

Guided Introspection – Forgiveness

So, why not experience this first hand for yourself? If you have the companion CD you can put it on now, or, you can have a friend read this and do it with them as a shared process.

Just find a comfortable position and when you're ready you can close your eyes.

First, bring all your awareness to this moment . . . Notice the sounds in the room . . . the feeling of your breath gently going in . . . and going out . . . And just let your whole being settle.

Make your heart as wide as the world . . . wide enough to include all the acts of hurt, blame and unforgiveness that have taken place in your life . . . Your love is so vast that you can even include all of humanity's unforgiveness.

Allow your awareness to expand spaciously in front . . . and vastly behind . . . infinitely to all sides . . . and just rest now as a vast open sky of all acceptance.

Into this sky really welcome memories, people and incidents that have taken place where you have felt unfairly treated, misjudged, hurt, trampled on or betrayed . . . Really put out a prayer of welcome for any time you've felt unforgiving to come into consciousness . . . All is welcome in this vast embrace.

If you'd like, you can also bring your awareness to your body and scan it . . . noticing any areas that seem a little tense, or stressed, or contracted . . . Notice if any parts are hiding . . . If so, welcome them, too . . . Let your love, your full awareness, surround that area and simply ask, 'If there were a feeling or words here, what would they be?' . . . Just welcome whatever feeling is here . . . even if it's as quiet as a whisper . . . Just allow all the feeling to come flooding . . . and ask, 'When have I felt like this before?' . . . and silently welcome any pictures or previous memories into your awareness . . . 'When have I felt like this before?' . . . Or you can just call into consciousness some time in the past when you've been the victim of unfair treatment or action – where you've felt hurt or judged by someone else.

When a memory, or a series of memories, has presented itself, allow yourself to imagine a beautiful campfire. The nature of this campfire is unconditional love, all acceptance.

To this campfire you can invite a younger you, age range zero until now . . . is the younger you there? . . . Good . . . Now invite the present day you – the you sitting here right now . . . And now you might like to invite a mentor of your own choosing – it could be a sage, a saint or an enlightened master – someone in whose divine wisdom you trust and in whose presence you feel safe . . . Are they all there? . . . Good.

Now it's time to invite the other person or people from that hurtful memory, when you felt wronged, or unfairly judged.

Is that person there? . . . Good.

Now I'd like to ask you to be very open and real here. If you are on your own or working with another person, you still need to voice *out loud* all the old repressed, unexpressed feelings that you never had a chance to express. This is your opportunity to finally release all that old pain, to finally get it all off your chest and out of your cells.

So it's time to let the younger you speak. The younger you has been through a lot of previously unexpressed pain, hurt and upset, and now at last it is time to let it all up and out. So, if the younger you could finally speak openly from *how you really felt at that time,* what would the younger you say? Give yourself the time needed to allow it all to come out – knowing that the other person is protected by the acceptance and love at the fire. Let your words penetrate to that 'deeper' place inside them, so they can hear what needs to be heard.

So, speaking from the pain, what might the younger you say? . . . (Give time)

And knowing that the other person was probably doing the best they could with the conditioning of their past and the internal resources they had at the time, if they could respond from that deeper place, what might they respond? . . . (Give time)

And if the younger you could respond to their words, what would you say? . . . (Give time)

And if the other person was able to really hear these words and were to respond not from ego, but from some place deeper, what might they respond? . . . (Give time)

What would the younger you reply to that? . . . (Give time)

Keep emptying out and conversing in this way until you both are completely empty . . . (Give time) – And just let me know when that feels complete . . . (Give time)

Now if the present day you could finally say what needs to be said, and if the other person could listen, what would the present day you say? . . . Great . . . (Give time)

And now let the other person respond . . . (Give time)

And how would you respond to that? . . . (Give time)

When both parties are completely emptied out, ask the mentor if there is anything he or she might like to say about all of this . . . And just let the mentor answer . . . (Give time)

If you like you can let the younger you step inside the body of the other person and really *feel* what they were feeling at the time . . . (Give time) How were they feeling about themselves? . . . About life? . . . Go even deeper . . . How did they *really* feel? . . . How were they secretly feeling inside, about themselves and about life?

Now step into their heart . . . into the very best part of them . . . into the part of them that they might not have had access to because they were feeling so bad, or were shut down. This part exists in all of us, for in our core there is a great love, peace, freedom . . . So step into their heart of hearts.

What is there? . . . (Give time) Now look out through their eyes at the younger you and feel how they were *really* feeling from their heart of hearts, from the level of their soul, at that time . . . (Give time)

How were they feeling? . . . (Give time) Can you see that their *behaviour* was born from the pain they were in at the time, but in their heart of hearts they felt positive, even loving, towards you?

Now step outside this person and let the younger you open your chest and receive a lifetime of their acceptance. Let it fill every cell. Then *divorce* from that love their actions, which were born from the pain of that time.

Now if they could finally speak to you from their deepest place inside what might they say? . . . (Give time)

What would you reply? . . . (Give time)

And what would they respond? . . . (Give time)

Make sure both of you have completely emptied out and come to full understanding . . . (Give time)

When all at the fire are completely emptied out, you can ask the younger you the following question: 'Even if you in *no* way condone the behaviour of the other person and even if their behaviour was totally unacceptable by society's standards and there is absolutely *no way* to condone it, are you willing to completely and utterly forgive that person with all of your heart?'

If the younger you says Yes, then let the younger you speak that forgiveness out truthfully, in your own words.

Then it is time to speak to the present day you and ask, 'Even if you in no way condone the behaviour, are you willing to completely and utterly forgive the other person with all of your heart?'

If the present day you says Yes, then let the present you forgive wholeheartedly, in your own words.

(If, by chance, the present you says 'No, I can't forgive' it simply means that you haven't emptied out completely, that more release is needed and you need to express anything, on any level, that you might be holding back. Once you are completely empty you can ask of the mentor, 'What would need to happen in order to forgive?' and then go ahead and let that take place here, at the campfire. Then proceed with the forgiveness of the other person.)

Then if *you* need forgiveness for anything, go ahead and receive it . . . (Give time)

And let all the people at the campfire merge into the light, sending your love and forgiveness and a prayer that they find peace in their lives.

Then turn to the younger you and say the following words: 'I'm so sorry for all the previous pain. You just didn't have access to all the wisdom that I do now. I promise you'll never have to go through that previous pain again, because from now on I will love and protect you.'

And then handing the younger you a balloon of self-love . . .

let the younger you breathe that in . . . Then a balloon of self-acceptance . . . breathing that in . . . and letting it suffuse your whole body . . . Then self-forgiveness . . . breathing that in . . . and letting it permeate you . . . Great . . .

Then hug the younger you and let the younger you merge inside, growing up now with all these beautiful internal resources, wisdom and forgiveness. Feel them permeating your whole body.

Now you can let the campfire disappear and you and your mentor can begin to feel your awareness expanding again . . . becoming vast and open in front . . . free and expansive behind . . . infinite to all sides . . . vast below . . . sky-like above . . . And once again, just rest as an open sky of freedom.

And you'll find that you'll be able to open your eyes only as soon as all parts of you are fully integrated and ready to carry on this healing and forgiveness starting now. And when all parts of you *are* fully integrated you'll find that you *will* be able to open your eyes now when you are ready, and experience the healing embrace of forgiveness in the room. Just rest in the freshness of the present moment.

So how are you feeling? If you were innocent and real in your emptying out, when it came time for forgiveness, it should have felt easy, obvious – almost choiceless – like it was the simplest and most natural thing to do.

Check your body and being right now. Can you feel the palpable sense of ease, relief and peace?

When *true* forgiveness takes place, the effects are instantaneous and they never miss their mark. It's a truth that can not be denied.

Forgiveness is a gift you give to yourself.

☆ ☆ ☆

Once you've done the campfire forgiveness process several times, there usually comes a time when the flashlight doesn't just point outwards – it turns back in your direction.

In the beginning most of our forgiveness work is outer directed. We are letting go of all the past ways that we've been wronged by others, how we've been cheated by life, or even forsaken by God. So the blame is projected outwards. And the forgiveness is of people or circumstances outside us. Then, over time, we run out of people and incidents to blame and eventually life requires us to look at ourselves and see the things *we've* done that we're not so proud of. Life requires us to look at words we've said that we wish we could take back, and examine hurtful actions we've done that we deeply regret. These campfires can be by far the most intense, but also the most profoundly healing.

Most of us are even harder on ourselves than we are on our loved ones. In a standard campfire process we may find ourselves quick to forgive others and let go, but when it comes to self-forgiveness we become harsh on ourselves, even cruel. We can have a tendency not to want to let ourselves off the hook so easily: it's as if we play God and judge. Yet for true healing we simply must forgive ourselves.

I really want to encourage you to do a few campfires like the one at the end of the Present-Moment Awareness chapter and go through a full emptying-out session and a complete forgiveness process with yourself. The greatest healing of all comes from self-forgiveness. It's time to give yourself that gift.

You'll find that when you're able to forgive yourself, forgiving others flows easily, effortlessly, naturally. And living in a bath of acceptance and compassion becomes as natural as breathing.

✲ ✲ ✲

My prayer is that in reading this chapter you realise that freedom is always available when you choose to forgive and let go. And it is a gift you can offer to every area of your life. It's something you *choose* to do and participate *in*, not something that is done to you.

Freedom and healing lie in your own hands. And it all begins with forgiveness.

There is an insidious kind of unforgiveness that most of us aren't even aware of. We make internal, unvoiced vows, that 'we're never going to forgive' so-and-so and then we forget that we've made them, and the vows go on to have a life of their own. Can you remember how, as a child, when someone hurt you or called you names, you may have innocently shouted inside your head, 'I'm never going to let that person hurt me again?' Or perhaps you promised, 'No one is ever going to get to me!' Or, 'I'm never going to let that person into my heart, ever!' On and on. Usually the vows begin with, 'I'm never . . .' or, 'So-and-so is not going to . . .' Especially if we made them with some intensity of feeling, these vows can go on to have a path of their own long after we've forgotten them, and they can be quite destructive. Then as adults we don't understand why we're not letting our partner get close to us and can't feel deep intimacy; we don't understand why we seemingly have a wall up against life and can't feel the 'juice,' or why our heart feels boxed and hidden away and why we are unable to fully feel real love. It's often because we've made a vow that is perpetuating itself in consciousness, and it's rising as an impulse at an other-than-conscious level.

Such vows usually have some element of unforgiveness in them and they can be seriously damaging to the relationships that you want to be open, intimate and true in (and this can include the relationship you have with yourself).

So, I'd like to conclude this chapter on forgiveness by offering you a guided introspection that allows you to discover and clear out unhealthy vows. It helps you to recognise the unhealthy vows that have been made and give you the chance to replace them with healthy, empowering and freeing vows. And mainly it frees you from any unvoiced unforgiveness going on at an other-than-conscious level.

✲ ✲ ✲

Guided Introspection – Changing Vows

If you have the companion CD you can use it for this process. Otherwise, it's probably best to get a friend to read this to you – that way you'll be able to relax deeply and surrender fully to the exercise.

So, let yourself find a comfortable position . . . and when

you are ready, you may close your eyes . . . take a nice deep breath in . . . and slowly let it out . . . and another long deep breath in . . . and slowly let it out . . . just relaxing and opening your being . . .

And as you continue to relax and open . . . imagine that in front of you is a downward-facing staircase . . . and this shimmering staircase has five steps . . . these are magical steps for they will lead you deeply into the light of your own being . . . into your essence . . . so, stepping now onto the top step, number five . . .

And relaxing in the knowledge that each step will effortlessly take you deeper into your own Self . . . stepping down onto step four . . . opening down to three . . . deeper down to two . . . and before you step onto the final step, step one . . . let your awareness expand infinitely in front . . . and behind . . . feeling consciousness become boundless to each side . . . opening spaciously above . . . and deepening ocean-like beneath . . . then step into the core of your own deepest awareness . . . as you step down onto step one now . . . and just rest at this awareness . . .

Now notice that to one side of you there is a doorway, and behind that doorway is the great light of your own soul . . . also waiting here is a mentor . . . one in whose divinity and wisdom you can trust . . . So now, when you're ready, walk through the doorway, into the light . . . and greet your mentor . . . thank him or her for being here to support you in changing an old vow that no longer supports you . . .

And now to the side is a very special vehicle . . . this is a time shuttle that will take you back to a time and place when a specific vow was made . . . a vow that has become inappropriate, or unhealthy, or unsupportive to the person you are today . . . So you and your mentor can step right into the shuttle, take a seat and fasten your seat belts . . . Then look at the dashboard in front of you . . . and see the blue button marked 'old vow' . . . know that when you press this button, the shuttle will take you safely and elegantly back in time . . . back to the time and the consciousness of that old vow . . . And either you or the mentor can press the blue button now . . . and let the shuttle take you where *it* knows to go . . . and when you arrive at the scene just allow the shuttle to come in for a soft gentle landing, and you can let me know that you've safely arrived . . . (Give time) . . . Great . . .

Now, you and your mentor can undo your seat belts and leave the shuttle, walking right back into the scene where the old vow was made . . . and you can also bring a guardian angel right here with you, if that feels helpful or appropriate . . .

Now take a moment to notice who else is here in the scene . . . and you can adjust the lighting level and the clarity of the scene until it's ideal . . . So, who else is here? (Give time to answer) . . . Good . . . Thank you . . . Now allow a campfire to appear right here in this scene . . . Know that this fire is the fire of unconditional love . . . of life itself . . . And bring also to this campfire the presence of God, or the presence of the infinite or the universe . . . and ask either the younger you in the scene or the mentor . . . What unhealthy vow was made here? . . . What vow was made that is no longer appropriate or supportive in this life stream? . . .

Then, in the knowledge that God, the infinite, the universe understands fully why this vow was initially made . . . and that it is no longer appropriate to leave it in place . . . Ask for blessings and assistance to undo and remove the old vow . . . and to replace it with a new healthy, wholesome vow . . . And when those blessings have been given, just let me know . . . (Give time) . . . Great . . . What old vow did you make? . . . What was the wording? . . . Great. Thank you.

So, now turn to the person or people in this scene, and let them know what vow was previously made . . . and why it is no longer appropriate to have this old vow in place . . . (Give time) . . . Let them know that it is your intention to let go of the old vow and replace it with a new, healthy vow . . . (Give time) . . . Good . . .

Now go ahead and forgive those at the campfire for playing their part in the making of the old vow . . . And ask for forgiveness from God, the infinite, the universe for anything that needs forgiving . . . and allow forgiveness to come to you from all those at the campfire . . . And you can let me know when this is complete . . . (Give time) . . . Good . . .

Now, turn to the mentor and ask that the old vow be swept clean . . . be completely cleared out from every cell of your being . . . Let the mentor sweep, wash, hose, vacuum away every vestige of that old vow . . . and you just watch and feel as that old vow is cleared from every molecule of your being . . . from all of consciousness . . . And you can just let me know when that's completely finished . . . (Give time) . . . Great . . .

And now ask the mentor to cut any ties or energetic cords that may attach you to the person or people in this scene . . .

make sure that healing light is sent through both ends of the ties as they are cut . . . Look into the faces of those who are being freed . . . Notice how grateful they are to be set free . . . Beautiful . . .

And now turn again to the mentor, and asking for assistance in the formulation of a new, healthy, appropriate vow . . . one that will empower you to be open, healthy, fulfilled and free . . . free to be your true Self . . . free to soar . . . And when you are ready, you can let me know what the new, healthy vow is . . . (Give time to answer, give assistance if needed) . . . That's beautiful . . . Thank you . . . So now just ask the mentor to install this brand new vow into every cell of your being . . . ask the mentor to flood every particle of your being with this new, empowering vow . . . making it an integral part of you . . . revitalising you . . . energising you . . . letting you come to peace and completion . . . (Give time) . . . And just let me know when this is completely complete . . . (Give time) . . . Beautiful . . .

So, in the knowledge that this new vow can only get stronger and more supportive over time . . . and knowing that it will heal and guide perfectly and naturally, of its own accord, without you having to do or think a thing . . . you can send blessings to all those at the campfire, thanking them for being here . . . and allowing them to merge into the fire that is the source of all life . . . Only you, the younger you and your mentor remain . . . Wonderful . . . Then let the younger you hug and merge with the present you . . . let the younger you grow up through all the intervening years with this new, empowering, healthy vow already in place . . .

sense the changes in consciousness that take place as the old integrates with the new . . . right up to the present time . . . And you can let me know when this is complete . . . (Give time) . . . Good . . .

Turn to the mentor and ask if there is any more teaching to be learnt here . . . if there is any insight or wisdom to be revealed . . . and if there is, just let that be revealed now . . . (Give time) . . . Good . . .

And now this is complete, you and your mentor can get back into the shuttle . . . and let the shuttle take you right back to the doorway you first came through . . . And when you arrive, just get out and thank your mentor with all your heart for being here in support of this life-changing process of release and healing . . . (Give time) . . . And then just step back to the doorway and walk over to the staircase you originally came down . . .

Now just step back up the steps . . . one . . . coming back to the present time . . . two . . . feeling refreshed and renewed . . . three . . . stretching and becoming more aware of your body . . . four . . . And now step into the future a day from now . . . and feel how you feel a day from now, with this brand new, empowering vow already a part of you . . . Great . . . And now step one week into the future . . . and see and hear and feel how it is to be the new you one week from now . . . Notice how differently you feel and how differently you are communicating with yourself and with others . . . Great . . . And now step into the future one month from now . . . and feel your being as it is flooded with the consciousness of the brand new you one month from now . . . How is it to be the new, free you? How does it feel to be released, healed and whole? . . . Fabulous! And now step six months into the future . . . and get a full sense of how your life is . . . how it is to have been free from that old, ancient vow for six months now . . . with the new, wholesome vow having done its work effortlessly for a full six months . . . So how does it feel to be free, to soar? . . . Great!

And know that time is just a concept . . . and that anything that appears in consciousness is already here . . . just allow the consciousness of the you six months from now to come back to the present moment . . . on step four . . . and know that you will only be able to step up onto step five and open your eyes when all parts of you are fully integrated in the knowledge that this healing, this release, this freedom can only grow and integrate organically . . . perfectly naturally, of its own accord . . . And when all parts are fully integrated and agreed then you may step up onto step five . . . And you can open your eyes now, when you are ready . . .

Congratulations!

enlightenment

The enlightenment you are seeking
is already embracing you, suffusing you.
It is shining as your Self.

When all ideas and concepts about it fall away,
what remains is pure, unobscured awareness . . .
enlightenment itself.

You are that.

While writing this book, I have known for some time that this chapter would eventually have to be written. With this knowing came an increasing reluctance to bring the topic onto the page, because I knew that as soon as the word enlightenment is mentioned all kinds of notions spring to mind. It is such a controversial word, and it seems that each and every spiritual aspirant or seeker has a different, yet equally certain definition or idea of what they *think* it *should* be and what it should look like. Many people aspire to attain this ultimate state or to have a sustained experience of it, but no one can even agree on what it is! The mind boggles with the myriad concepts and ideas that arise with the mere welcoming of this word into consciousness. Yet, welcome it we must.

Even in the simple reading of the word 'enlightenment', many of you may already have had numbers of images come to mind. Some of you might have imagined a wise, saffron-robed sage, with a beatific expression, sitting in a perfect yogic lotus posture, and seeming entirely removed from worldly aspirations. Often, with that picture comes the false belief that these enlightened beings are always and eternally established in bliss, in peace – and that no emotion could even create a ripple in their sublime stillness.

Others of us, never having seen a so-called enlightened master, might not have a clue what enlightenment looks like; but we still hold out a belief that it must mean the end of all suffering, all judgements, indeed, the end of anything that is not what *we* consider enlightened thinking or enlightened behaviour.

For others there is a belief that enlightenment means you must be totally free; not bound by any of the rules of society, and established in a benevolent love that allows you to act freely, lovingly towards all beings; and that no negative thought or belief could possibly penetrate this presence of grace.

Still others hold the belief that in order to be enlightened you must annihilate the ego, penetrate the lie of the worldly illusion and, in one cataclysmic event you suddenly are enlightened – and you remain that way for the rest of your life. It is as if some huge magical, liberative blasting has to take place, and then suddenly you *land* in final enlightenment. Some spiritual teachers have even come to label this experience as 'smashing the pot' or receiving the 'final cut'.

Yet others of us believe that enlightenment is only for the rare masters who have spent their lives in spiritual austerities, learning all the rituals, mantras, yogas, scriptures, purifying their minds and bodies. They finally attain enlightenment – something almost completely unavailable and unattainable by the normal, everyday householder.

For others enlightenment looks like total detachment, as if the teacher is entirely, almost inhumanly disengaged from life; not responding in any way to the everyday sufferings that beset the rest of humanity. This version of enlightenment usually includes the notion of 'transcending' worldly life, and such a master will appear emotionless, almost lifeless.

Then there is the belief that if you are enlightened you must live your life in poverty and complete austerity, spending your outer-world actions in good deeds and in helping others to awaken to their own purity.

Some people even believe that with enlightenment come the super-human powers of mind reading, seeing into the future, astral projection and other 'siddhis'; and that with enlightenment, all desires are magically fulfilled, and that disease cannot visit the body of the holy one.

On and on and on . . . our mental constructs pile up, as we try to imagine and project what it must be like to live in this ultimate state of bliss, paradise, nirvana. All of our ideas coagulate around, distort and magnify this notion called enlightenment, until the whole thing seems so impossible, so distant – something that could only be attained at some far off time in the future, after having spent a lifetime doing everything we could to *earn* it and *attain* it.

Do you recognise what I am talking about?

* * *

Guided Introspection – Enlightenment

What ideas have *you* brought with you regarding enlightenment?

Why not let them come into your awareness right now? As a matter of fact, welcome every concept you've ever had about the subject of enlightenment and, if you like, you can write them down on a piece of paper, including all your descriptions and all your ideas about their attainability.

Once you are completely emptied out, and everything you believe is true about enlightenment has been brought into consciousness, ask yourself, 'What if I were to discover it was *all a lie* . . . just a load of bullshit?'

What if *all* notions, ideas and concepts were, in fact, *just that* . . . just ideas born from a mental construct of a projected ideal that you wish for or aspire to – something that you long to 'get' one day? What if everything you imagined to be true about enlightenment turned out to be, in fact, just some fantasy born from a deep wish to experience the divine, the sublime, the infinite? What if every notion you ever held regarding enlightenment was just a dream? And what if the very act of creating these imaginary constructs and mental images was *preventing* you from experiencing the unobscured enlightenment that is *already* here – the vast, boundless, infinite presence which is your own essence?

What if there was *nothing* to attain? – What if you are already resting in an ocean of enlightened awareness, and can't see It because you're too busy looking for something 'out there' – that ideal, that paradise, that nirvana – instead of opening into the infinite presence that is already waiting here, calling you *home* to yourself?

What if there was nothing you could *do* to attain enlightenment? And what if enlightenment is only revealed in the *not doing,* in effortless being?

Try an experiment right now. Imagine taking *all* your notions, images and mental constructs and putting a huge red 'X' right through them. If you write them down on paper you can do exactly that. Then imagine bundling all those beautifully crafted concepts into a nice sack and, in your mind's eye, burning them. Or, if you've written them on paper, you could literally burn them, or rip them up and toss them in the bin.

Once all constructs have disappeared, all mind talk is gone, all idyllic notions have dissolved . . . when all ideas have vanished . . . what remains?

Really *experience* this – even if for just one moment. Just take a moment to be still . . . Experience what it is like when consciousness is free from all mental activity . . . Stop . . . breathe . . . Just give yourself *one* moment, without any idea about anything . . . Just experience thought-free awareness.

What remains? . . . What is left when all thought has come and all thought has gone? . . . What truly remains? And is this vast spacious awareness touched in any way by the ideas that have come and gone through it? . . . Or does it just remain totally free, whole, complete?

Check for yourself . . . when all thoughts have been welcomed, and naturally fade away . . . what remains?

If you are really innocent and open . . . if you take a moment to pause . . . breathe . . . be still . . . you will experience unobscured freedom, nothingness, vastness . . . pure presence . . . enlightened awareness.

Enlightened awareness is experienced as being here when all thoughts, constructs and ideas have been removed, let go of. It is revealed to be the wide, open field *in which* all thoughts appear and disappear.

You didn't have to do any mantras or practices, or perform any great austerities or 'sadhana' to get this – for this open presence is your own nature: it's already whole; it's already completely attained! As a matter of fact, any efforting to *try* to attain it only pushes the direct experience of it further into the distance.

It's only when you *stop* . . . breathe . . . open . . . welcome all thought – really welcome it . . . that thought is free to come to rest. It's free to come and it's free to go; and *you* can rest in the vast, open presence through which it is appearing.

Something is welcoming thought . . . some huge, empty presence is the welcomer. That presence is your own self, your own essence – and any mental constructs, beliefs, mind talk or images that come through it are simply that . . . thoughts – a bunch of words and images travelling through consciousness.

You *are* the consciousness through which all is coming and all is going. So, whether those ideas are right or wrong doesn't matter – they are just some syllables trailing through awareness, through the boundless freedom that you already are.

Enlightenment is always here, always available. It is who *you are*.

I remember hearing a delightful story that drove home to me how fruitless and useless it is to go searching for enlightenment, when it is already here. This is an old story that is often passed down from teacher to student, and I have heard variations of it from various teachers, but it is always a fresh reminder to call off the search and experience what is here right now.

So, once again, you might like to get comfortable, relax . . . and feel yourself opening to read a story that will remind you of the ocean of grace that you are already resting *in*.

> Once upon a time, there was a very young, playful and characterful wave. This wave was full of fun, and loved to bubble and effervesce and dance in various circular motions. It delighted totally in its wave-like existence, and simply loved to play.
>
> One day, the young wave was making some particularly mischievous movements when he heard a deep, almost imperceptible sound coming from the very depths . . . 'ocean' . . . it said.
>
> Upon hearing this deep, resonant sound, something began to stir in the wave's being, and he felt a strong pull from the most primal part of himself to understand its meaning. It sounded compellingly mysterious, and the young wave just couldn't stop thinking about it.
>
> His thirst to understand this mystery began to grow and, as a dolphin was passing near by, the young wave asked for some advice, 'Oh, dolphin, before you go – you've always seemed so smart, so clever – can you tell me something? I heard that

there is something called "ocean," only I don't know what it means, or where it is. Can you tell me?'

The dolphin squeaked back that he'd been hearing everyone talk about it for some time, and that there were a few theories floating around about what it must be like – there were even some older, scholarly dolphins who took regular meetings to try to understand its meaning – but no one had yet discovered the truth of it: the concept was still at the ideas stage.

The dolphin wished the young wave blessings and flipped his flipper goodbye, as he laughed and frolicked out of sight. Just as he was disappearing from view, he shouted, 'Good luck. Maybe you'll be the first one to discover the great mystery.' And then he disappeared.

Later that day an old, wise turtle came drifting by and the young wave perked up and asked the ancient one the same question. Figuring that this old tortoise had probably grown wise in his long years, the wave hoped he might know the answer to his mystery.

'Oh turtle, surely you've travelled and seen much over your many years. And I am but a young wave, and have not the benefit of your experience . . . so, please . . . can you tell me . . . have you ever heard of the ocean? . . . Have you ever seen it? Every time I hear the word arising inside, it stirs something deep within. I *must* come to understand it, to experience it. Please can you help me, old wise one?'

The turtle listened quietly to the impetuous wave, and answered in a slow, low voice, 'Oh son, that is a question I myself have been pondering for, lo, these many years . . . but, honestly, I can't say I've ever seen it. I can't even say I know what it is. I sense there is a deep secret, and many have developed complex theories about its nature, but I can't say that I've actually got any real knowledge of it. No son, like me, I fear you may spend the rest of your days searching for the answer.

'I wish you good fortune, young one. You have your whole life ahead of you; perhaps you'll be the rare and lucky one to find the true experience of the ocean . . .'

The young wave felt saddened that he was having so little success with his quest to find the ocean, and he feared that maybe no one could really give him an answer.

The next day a big, old, well-formed wave came rolling in his direction. Excited, thinking that surely this majestic grandfather wave *must* have his answer, the little wave asked spiritedly, 'Oh, great wave – you are old and wise, and have lived much longer than someone as young as I. I've heard a rumbling from somewhere deep inside, and the word *ocean* keeps haunting me. I *have* to find it. I simply *must* find the answer to my mystery. What is it? Where can I find it?'

The old wave sighed a deep sigh . . . 'Oh, young one . . . this is a question that only the wisest of the wise ask. You must be a very special wave, that you have such a deep spiritual calling to understand the mysteries of the ocean . . . I wish I could help you . . . but I have been travelling all of my days, and this thirst for the ocean – to find it, to know its meaning – has never left me and, try as I might, I've never fathomed its mystery . . .

'Oh, many have conjectured and *thought* they had figured

it out, and others have constructed all their complicated theories. Everyone agrees that the truth of it must be nearly impossible to attain, but I've certainly never experienced it. In all honesty, I'm not even sure it really exists.'

The little wave sank in disappointment and, sensing how sad the young wave had become, the big wave made a bold invitation. 'Listen, young one . . . Why don't you travel with me? If we go on this quest together, perhaps the mystery will finally unfold; maybe the secret will be revealed. The older I get, of course, the larger I get, but also the simpler I get. I just can't cotton on with all these highfalutin' theories about what it must mean. I keep feeling in the very depths of my being that the presence of the ocean is very close – if only I could grasp it.

'Let's travel together, and we'll see what life brings us.'

And so they did: the young perky, playful wave building its strength and volume, as it travelled alongside the great old wise wave.

After many miles they both began to feel a current from deep within, and sensed that their journey was quickening. In complete surrender they let themselves open into the power that was mysteriously building from the depths.

Then they spied, way in the distance, something never before experienced, but something they'd heard whispered about between the fishes. The old wave said, 'My goodness! That must be what the fishes are referring to when they speak of the shore, and the land beyond. I never thought I'd actually see it in my lifetime!'

The power inside became even stronger, and as they came closer and closer to the shore a compelling surge seemed to be driving them both faster, and faster . . . faster . . . faster toward the beach. They picked up more and more speed until, suddenly, *crash*! . . . All bubbling, foaming, splashing . . . they openly surrendered, and they both merged into the ocean from where they'd come. In an instant the realisation was there: they'd always *been* the ocean – it was their very essence. They were made from it. They were infused with the infinite presence of it. It had always been their true nature. It was just that in the past they'd only identified with being the wave *on top* of the ocean, never realising that they'd always been and always would be the vast, boundless ocean itself.

✲ ✲ ✲

You are this ocean. You *are* the very enlightenment you have been seeking.

It's time to call off the search, and just rest in the infinite presence that has always been and will always be *who you already are.*

Let the whole play of mind come to dance on your surface. Even though thoughts, like waves, arise from the ocean of being, they are *not* the ocean itself. Instead, like waves, they are free to come and free to go: the depths of the ocean remain completely undisturbed by all the drama of life parading through it. You are the ocean – the infinite ocean of enlightenment.

Like this little wave, and like many spiritual seekers around the world, I too spent most of my younger years thirsting, seeking, longing to experience enlightenment, to merge into the divine. I went from teachers, to masters, to yogis, to monasteries, to ashrams. I traversed many spiritual traditions, read all the right texts, did endless austerities, fasts, practices, mantras – all in an effort to find freedom, to slake this seemingly unslakeable thirst to experience that infinite presence as an ongoing, everlasting, direct realisation.

Along the way I learnt countless theories, and came to firmly believe that enlightenment could only be attained through endless practice, fervent desire, total surrender and complete focus on the goal one hundred per cent of the time. I sat with several enlightened masters and, in their wakeful presence, experienced countless awakenings and bathed in the bliss of freedom. Still I kept searching. Even in the midst of basking in scintillating presence, steeping in love, the longing still burned. Sometimes I thought I might die in the ferocity of its blaze – in fact, I was willing to physically die if it meant merging into God, realising Self, opening into the infinite, resting in enlightenment.

Grace was surrounding me, embracing me, shining in everything, but *still* I held onto the notion that enlightenment was to be *attained*, and was somewhere 'out there', and would happen at some time in the future.

I was pigeon-holing these sublime experiences, categorising them as mere passing states and relegating them to the past – renouncing the experience of it all as not *true* enlightenment, and letting it become another beautiful, faded memory. All my focus and attention was on my imagined goal. I was projecting myself into some ideal picture of what I *believed* enlightenment must be like, overlooking the infinite presence I was already steeped in!

Like the little wave, there I was already soaking in it – but I was still reaching outside, trying to find it, to experience it, to fathom its mystery. I had put myself on a path of postponement.

Then one day, like the wave I had a wonderful collision with reality, and a cataclysmic realisation crashed through my world of the known. In that one moment all my ideas fell away: my beliefs about who I thought I was, my identification with a constructed somebody I'd come to believe was my self – for one instant all the concepts of enlightenment completely dropped away. And in that moment I saw through the lie of my search.

When all identifications, beliefs, concepts and theories were gone, everything that had been obscuring open awareness became *obviously apparent.*

I'd overlooked the obvious because my focus had always been elsewhere! All along, this that I had been seeking was already *here*.

I realised that I was resting in an ocean of grace, pure presence, unobscured freedom, and I recognised that I'd spent my whole life in this embrace – I'd simply overlooked it! It wasn't somewhere 'out there', in my future. It was *right* here, surrounding, suffusing and shining in everything. And it was realised to be here the instant I got fully present to it. When I'd stopped labelling it as a past experience, stopped imagining what it might be like in the future; when I stopped all the mind games and just innocently opened into the present moment – unobscured awareness was realised to be here. In fact, I experienced it as being everywhere, *in* everything.

What a joke! All my life I spent in fruitless searching, when what I was seeking was closer than my own breath. And I didn't even have to *do* anything to get it. In fact, it was my very 'doing' that had taken me *away* from it!

From that day forward I ceased seeking and decided it was time to just relax – to rest in the open presence that is shining here, available each and every moment, whenever you bring your awareness to it.

I hadn't recognised it, but somehow I'd fostered a notion that enlightenment was a landing place – that you landed there and suddenly and forever you were enlightened, realised.

I didn't know then what I do now: that enlightenment is simply an invitation to open and be fully present in this moment – with no thought of past, and no thought of future – just this moment. And it's fully and completely available each time you bring your awareness to the now. It can't go anywhere because it is yourself. You can let your attention wander and let your mind collapse into some other notion or concept, but the moment you stop . . . open . . . and just be still, everything you are seeking is realised to be already here.

I came to realise that enlightenment is a continual opening: concepts can't cling to it, lies burn away in it, dramas get played out through it, and the whole dance of life is happening in it – waking, sleeping, all of life takes place in this vast embrace.

Sometimes, when my awareness collapses into some story, I still get lost in the drama of something 'out there' and I believe myself to be the wave – I get caught up in its unique movements and ever-changing patterns for a brief time and, in those moments, the ocean fades into the background and the drama on the surface takes centre stage. But the second I stop, drop the story and any belief in it, the ocean pulls me back into itself – into an endless sea of peace; and I realise its presence was there all along, even when I pretended for a moment to get involved in the game and played at being a little wave.

Of course, its presence is always here. How can the ocean go anywhere? It's what you are made of, who you are. Wherever you go, there it is – and all thoughts, dramas, the full dance of life are merely waves on the surface of this that is your infinite Self.

Since the day I penetrated the lie of my illusory search and realised that I am this ocean, it has become increasingly difficult to buy into the drama dancing on the surface for any length of time. For me, the reality of this moment and the power of its presence is too strong a pull to resist – it keeps calling me back into itself.

So these days I find the drama of life may still dance through – it just seems to be happening in a vaster presence of grace. Thoughts come and go in it, feelings are welcome in it – in fact, all of life is welcome in it – yet the infinite presence *does not* come and *does not* go.

It is time to call off the search.

You are this that you have been seeking.

✲ ✲ ✲

Yesterday, I ran into a radiant young man who appeared to be in his early twenties. He seemed to have a clear, sharp mind, and it was obvious that he was a fervent spiritual seeker.

He stopped me just as I was leaving my friend Isaac's house. I was in a rush to keep my appointment with grace, to continue writing this book, and I was already running late and didn't feel that I had time to spare for any additional conversation, but something in the young man's eyes made me stop, just as I had my foot out of the front door.

'Do you mind if I ask you a spiritual question?' he asked.

Internally, I scrambled. I'd already made up my mind to leave, and time was urging me forward. Hesitating, I took a moment to meet his intense eyes. There was a burning urgency there – a genuine longing to find some answer to a real spiritual question he had, and compassion flooded my being. He looked like I must have so often appeared to my teachers – thirsty, hungry, searching for true answers to deep questions.

I paused, then my heart melted and I replied, 'Well, we'll see what arises,' (knowing that all answers are only ever in the hands of grace, and truly not knowing whether I even had an answer to his question.)

'Is it possible we can make it brief?' I asked gently. 'I'm actually in a bit of a rush.'

I watched the young man as he struggled internally to find a way to make his question clear and succinct, to get right to the core of the issue. He stammered a bit, then it came tumbling out in a rush of words punctuated with pauses, stops and starts, 'In enlightenment . . . I mean when someone is enlightened . . . they don't have any preferences, do they? . . . I mean . . . they view everything as the same, don't they? . . . I mean . . . if they're *really* enlightened, they don't judge if something is different from something else . . . do they?'

I stood still, looking into his eyes, and was getting ready to reply, when more words came tumbling out. 'I mean, like when I go to the shopping mall . . . I prefer some things and I don't like others . . . and some things I see there are so commercial that I dislike them . . . and sometimes I see people doing things there that I don't think are right . . . and, well . . . judgement comes in. But, in enlightenment . . . I mean . . . does judgement ever arise in enlightenment . . . if you're *really* enlightened?'

He stumbled a bit more, trying to further articulate his question, until finally I asked, 'So, when you go to the mall . . . you find you have preferences and that judgement arises? Is that it?'

'Well, yes . . . but does it happen in enlightenment?'

Briefly, my mind touched on some memories of the various enlightened masters I'd sat with, and internally I smiled. They didn't just have preferences; they had *strong* preferences, and often expressed them loud and clear to all who would listen. But I answered, 'By enlightenment, you mean this vast, empty field of presence that is here?' I indicated a spaciousness with my hands, as if it were already surrounding us, embracing us.

'Well . . . yes. But do differences show up in it?'

'All kinds of preferences show up in it – judgements come and go; strong emotions come and go; likes and dislikes come and go, but this infinite presence . . .' (again I indicated with my hands a vastness of space) 'is not touched by anything.

'It sounds like you are *judging* your judgements . . . Are you?'

He nodded his head, as I saw something slotting into place.

'So, what if you stopped judging what came through this enlightenment? What if, instead, you welcomed all your judgements *into* it? Has it occurred to you that perhaps these judgements are longing for freedom, and that they are coming up for satsang, to taste enlightenment? Our judgements long for freedom, just like everything else does.

'What if you were to do something radical, right now? – Just stop for a moment – become aware of the spaciousness already here . . . and ask for all the judgements to come flooding? Really welcome them . . .'

For a moment he stared into space, as if his awareness had turned inward. Then his body visibly relaxed as he genuinely welcomed his judgements. While he was welcoming them I said, 'You know what? . . . Just welcome *all* judgements into this love, this freedom . . . not just those particular ones, but *all* of them . . . all of mankind's judgements . . . even your ancestors' judgements . . . Stay spacious . . . Stay open . . . Now, is enlightenment – is this spacious love touched by any of your judgements?'

'No . . . I get it . . . No, it's not.'

'Who is it that is welcoming the judgements?'

He visibly opened his being, and answered, 'I am.'

'Yes, you are the welcomer – you are the infinite field that is welcoming all judgement into spaciousness.

'So, when no resistance is here; when all welcome is here – is there any problem with judgements?' I asked.

'No . . .' he said, quite incredulously, 'No . . . no problem at all.'

'Perhaps your judgements just needed a little love. Perhaps all they needed was to be welcomed into the love. Are they any problem to this field of love?'

'No . . . not at all.'

'So, why don't you just *love* all your judgements? Just welcome them all into this love while you remain *as* this field of love – untouched by anything that comes through it.

'All kinds of things come through this enlightenment, you know – emotions, thoughts, judgements, preferences – but can you experience that this that you are is untouched by anything coming through?'

He opened further.

'Yes . . . yes, I can.'

'Well, I have an assignment for you. After I leave, go take a few minutes to sit quietly in this vast openness, and just welcome every judgement you've ever had into this love. Discover for yourself what *remains* untouched.

'Just love your judgements to death . . . Love them to death.'

He smiled at the metaphor, recognised its true meaning, nodded approval, and agreed that he would do exactly that after I left.

And I have no doubt that he did. And I'm sure he loved them to death.

This love is such a vast, open field – it makes no judgements about *what* comes through it, and as a result no resistance arises. It's only when you think something *shouldn't* be there, and try to push it away or judge it, that any resistance arises.

He *was* right. In enlightened awareness, love makes no distinction. It accepts all, and allows everything to come through – and it's unstained, untainted and untouched by any of it.

It just depends – do you identify with the thoughts and judgements, or do you open and let them pass through the vaster context of your being? The choice is yours: enlightenment is always present, always available, no matter what choices you make . . . it loves you that much.

✲ ✲ ✲

Judgement is not the only trap we get locked into. Without our realising it, an entire mental construct of certitude can arise regarding the nature of enlightenment and what it *looks* like. After many experiences of the infinite and after sitting countless times in the presence of a master, without our knowing, an arrogant expertise can arise. We can fall into the certain, absolute belief that we have become acutely discerning: we *know* what enlightenment *looks* like, what it's supposed to *feel* like, even what it's meant to *sound* like, and this very knowing can cause us to miss it when it's standing right before our eyes.

I definitely fell into that trap many years ago.

As a spiritual seeker, through the course of my life I was blessed to sit with many extraordinary teachers, and ended up spending seven years at the feet of a particularly sublime and radiant enlightened master – Gurumayi. In her presence, everything became alive with a scintillating grace. The very atmosphere seemed saturated with it. In her presence, even the most ordinary and simple of rooms would appear glorious, resplendent and permeated with peace.

Through the course of all those years, I had countless awakenings, revelations, experiences of bliss, realisations, and there was no doubt in my mind that I was sitting with a true master, in the presence of enlightenment.

I surrendered myself totally to that grace, and like many of her students, I learned how to serve truth in each moment as I offered all of myself in selfless service in her ashrams and centres.

I felt myself to be the luckiest person alive and, holding onto my concrete belief that enlightenment was available 'out there, some time in the future,' the ferocity of devotion to freedom only became fiercer and fiercer. The longing to merge into God, into grace, became almost unbearable. This longing was taking place even while I was resting in bliss. It would not cease. When I went to bed it was burning, when I awoke it was the first experience of the day.

My husband, who shared my great love of truth, had a thirst to experience self-inquiry (advaita), and wanted to learn from a true jani master. He had heard of an old enlightened master who had been 'fully realised' for over fifty years, and who lived in a very humble village north of Delhi in India.

The master was considered by many to be the final teacher. In his presence, many students were reported to have become liberated, and several enlightened teachers still came to sit with him, for his intellect was piercing, and he could penetrate any concepts or ideas of separation that might be surreptitiously hanging about in consciousness. Poonjaji, also affectionately known as Papaji, though living an extremely modest life, was reputed to be the final step in your journey to enlightenment.

But I felt completely graced in Gurumayi's presence, and did not share the same pull as my husband felt. So it was only out of marital devotion to him that I accompanied him to Lucknow, India to sit with this venerated teacher.

Whether Papaji's reputation was true or not, I didn't know. To me, these were only rumours after all. And ultimately, I secretly believed that no one could *really* attain enlightenment – that you had to have it *bestowed* upon you, as a final descent of grace from the teacher whom you'd spent years serving, and in whose presence, through practices and austerities, your being and body had become totally purified. Certainly, I fitted into that category, as my commitment to the practices were total. Though the possibility for full realisation existed, I believed it would ultimately come only through the teacher's grace.

My path was already chosen: my sadhana was firmly established in Gurumayi's teachings, and I was interested in no other master. She was my beloved teacher and I trusted her utterly, and lived her teachings as my life.

So, reluctantly, with little interest and mild scepticism, I went to see this great master Poonjaji in the north of India.

When we arrived in Lucknow; a place full of poverty, sickness, mangy dogs, pigs living in open sewers, horses worked until they were barely standing up, the air choked with pollution, I wondered, 'What the heck am I doing here?' Papaji's home is a suburb of Lucknow, and had nothing sublime about it. Though I'd been to India several times, and had grown to love it, to my western eyes, this village still looked like a cesspool.

I was used to sitting with Gurumayi in her Ganeshpuri Ashram in south India, which was an exquisite monastery, set in paradisiacal botanical gardens, picturesque, pristine, resplendent with devotion – not this filthy, grimy, stinking, impossibly hot village with no air to breathe.

The morning after we arrived, having found some lodgings locally, we ended up standing in a long queue to get into Papaji's satsang hall. Everyone was huddled around the front door, impatient to get into the small hall that could hold only 200 students, and it seemed to my eyes that no one had even bothered to dress for the occasion.

I was accustomed to long, orderly queues waiting for the master, where everyone was respectful and quiet with anticipation; always bathed, dressed in our Sunday best to honour the occasion and to show our respect – but this was at best a motley, dishevelled and disorganised group.

I wasn't impressed. I had my long list of rules and morals about how to behave around the master, and these people appeared not to know the simplest teachings of honouring themselves, each other or the teacher.

Like a teeming brawl we flooded through the front door. Pushing to find seats, everyone scrambled to get close to the front, and the satsang hall was completely packed with people sitting on a stone floor, knee to knee – practically in each other's laps. At one point we were asked to move as far forward as possible, to make room for others still standing outside the door, and so we all crammed together closely like so many sardines. Everyone's body was touching someone else's. I felt my space parameters uncomfortably encroached upon – people seemed to touch way too much for my more austere sensibilities. Nothing matched my vision of spiritual decorum.

My mind was flooded with nothing but judgements. 'Is this the way to behave in the presence of a venerated master?' I thought. I was so arrogant, so superior. I *knew for certain* the respectful protocol for sitting with a teacher, and to my eyes these bedraggled, hippy wanderers from around the world didn't have a clue how to behave.

Papaji entered the hall very quietly and unassumingly, without any fanfare, and a ripple went through the audience, and everyone settled and became still.

Papaji's demeanour was humble, open; not studied or practiced in any way. He seemed totally at ease, and laughed often and deeply. Most of what he said I had heard before, and I was somewhat shocked at some of the irreverent seeming questions asked by some of the students. Didn't they know who they were sitting with? Sitting with an enlightened master was the rarest, most priceless of experiences. These students seemed more fond of hearing their own voices than that of the master. The whole session seemed a shambles compared with the restrained, quiet, planned, orderly, pristine and formal satsangs I was accustomed to.

None of it matched my pictures *of how a seeker is meant to behave in the presence of a master.* And, because I was so full of all my preconceptions, I couldn't see the deep devotion burning in many people's eyes. I couldn't feel the still presence emanating from them, nor could I sense the power of their commitment to truth.

At the end of the session, we all stood. I was soaking in a blaze of burning stillness, and we put our hands in prayer position and namastéd Papaji as he left the hall. As he was passing by he looked me deeply in the eyes, and then turned to my husband and spontaneously invited us to lunch at his home.

Shocked, nonplussed, I looked at the other students around me. Wasn't he going to invite them? It appeared not. I felt a little embarrassed and on the spot, yet simultaneously blessed beyond words. We followed him to his car, waved goodbye, and then walked down the dusty road to his house.

His living room/dining room area was simpler than any I'd ever seen – just a plain Formica topped table with a plastic tablecloth and old chairs from the 50s. On the floor, around the walls of what was a tiny lounge, were ordinary, somewhat worn and unmatched cushions. A flickering fluorescent lamp lit this spartan room; its only distinguishing decorative features being some pictures of places and saints that Papaji had gathered on his many travels.

Papaji, who was eighty-two years old, hobbled to his dining table, and quietly read through the stack of letters from ardent seekers asking spiritual questions. He motioned for my husband and me to sit down at the end of the table, asked a few polite-seeming questions about how we'd come to meet him, and then turned his attention back to his mail. Finally, lunch arrived and we ate a simple, lovingly prepared meal, without any prayers or special offerings.

Perhaps you may not have had the opportunity to sit with a spiritual master in your life, but most of us have been bombarded by images: movies like *The Little Buddha*; *The Last Samurai*; *Crouching Tiger, Hidden Dragon*; *Samsara*; *Himalaya*; *Seven Years in Tibet*, and newsreels of the Dalai Lama; the David Carradine Kung-Fu television series from the 70s – we all have our own images of a monk sitting quietly in a sacred space, dressed in robes, absorbed in silence, espousing carefully chosen words of deep and profound wisdom.

But Papaji did not fit into this picture at all. He'd changed out of his traditional kurta, (a simple long shirt with a Nehru collar and matching white trousers) and was now wearing a clean, though somewhat tattered T-shirt bearing the words BYRON BAY. I figured someone must have given it to him long before, perhaps to entice him to visit Australia. There was nothing glamorous, monk-like or ascetic about him. He looked so *ordinary*, so plain – like your grandfather might if he were sitting in his old T-shirt at his kitchen table.

Yet this was the 'teachers' teacher', the gurus' guru. It didn't make any sense to my *eyes*.

Above us, on the wall behind his table, was an old-fashioned television set that someone must have given him – one that frequently went on the blink, as did most of the electricity in the house from time to time. No sacred halls, no quietly robed monks serving him, no pomp or circumstance – just an old man sitting in a modest room in an impoverished Indian village.

Papaji invited us to stay at his house for our entire visit and, as he was currently on a special fast in honour of one of the holy celebrations of his tradition, we joined him in that austerity. We ate only raw fruit and vegetables, (washed in disinfectant as this was India) and this was fine for me, as I had done many fasts in my life.

Why we were invited I didn't know. What we were supposed to learn wasn't apparent. Although he gave daily satsang at the meeting hall, Papaji wasn't giving any formal teachings at the house, so we were just sitting watching an octogenarian go about living a quiet, mundane-seeming life.

At times Papaji seemed to get grumpy. In the next moment, he might laugh to himself about something ironic he'd just read in a letter. Irritation came and went. Impatience arose and subsided. If a letter arrived that was deeply moving, he would sit and cry at the beauty of it. The whole panoply of human emotion seemed to play through his consciousness. Yet, like an infant who feels emotion freely and easily, none of it seemed to stick. It was as if the emotion arose, was felt and passed cleanly through; and the stillness remained untouched by it.

Day after day we sat quietly. Sometimes we spoke, sometimes people came to deliver things and were invited in, but as we were on a fast, he didn't invite others in for meals. So it was just a handful of people preparing raw food, cleaning, tending to the needs of the house, while Papaji sat in silence or watched cricket and wrestling on Indian television. Sometimes, a movie on the Ramayana or Mahabharata would come on as a special programme in the evening, but there was nothing remarkable-seeming about any of it. Everything was so human, so real, so normal.

It was on the fifth day of our fast, and we were sitting in silence, when suddenly the thought arose, 'What am I doing here in this house watching an old man who has a penchant for loud Indian television?' Then the next thought arose, 'Oh, my God – that's the first thought I've had in five days!'

I had been resting so quietly in thought-free awareness that it hadn't even occurred to me to question it . . . it was so natural, so unremarkable, so ordinary – as if resting in pure presence had always been the only experience I had ever known. There was no running commentary going on internally, no mental grasping, grappling, resisting or ideation. I was saturated in pure peace, and I hadn't even noticed it because my thinking mind had come to rest and there was no one there to comment on it; just pure awareness being itself.

There hadn't been some huge thunderbolt, or any crashing experience of awakening. I was just resting in thought-free stillness, and it was as natural as brushing my teeth.

All of my ideas of what enlightenment 'looked' like: how we had to behave, be; what one should do, ought to do, had melted away into nothingness; and I was just left as pristine awareness.

It was at the end of the fast that I finally put pen to paper and wrote a letter to Papaji, begging for final enlightenment – I wanted to merge into God. It seemed partly absurd, because who would merge into what I didn't know – for everything was alive as consciousness. But, somehow I still held on to this old concept that I needed a final blasting realisation, and grace bestowal in order to attain enlightenment, so that is what I asked for.

What took place over the next several days was not just the experience of a one-off blasting realisation, but more a simple stripping away of all the lies, illusions, identifications, fantasies, judgements, rules, beliefs and concepts that I had about enlightenment. Patiently, Papaji peeled away all the concepts, until all that remained was pure awareness. Sometimes, he turned my acquired knowledge upside down and inside out, until we both just laughed at the absurdity of them. At other times, he asked me to inquire into the reality, into the truth of the nature of my ideas and beliefs, and they were seen to be nothing but empty concepts that seemed to be totally insubstantial.

At other times, when I was speaking about previous revelations and powerful kundalini experiences, he would ask, 'Are these experiences here right now?'

'No, Papaji,' I would answer, and he would reply, 'This that comes and this that goes is *not real*. You abide in this that *always* remains – in reality: in the eternal presence that does not come and does not go.'

Like so many sandcastles, the concepts dissolved, until the whole notion that there ever *was* a separate somebody called Brandon came into question. That, too, was realised to be just another idea – and when the lie of that illusion was penetrated, all the legs holding up the table called 'enlightenment' finally collapsed, and the game of believing in an enlightenment 'out there' was finished.

It wasn't that he gave me some huge, final teaching. It was that he penetrated all the lies and limitations I'd created regarding enlightenment. It was not a time of addition, but one of subtraction. Instead of *giving* me teachings, practices, mantras and beliefs, *he took them all away*. And what remained was unobscured awareness, pure presence, radiant emptiness.

He told me that the only difference between one who is enlightened and one who is not is belief: the certain belief that you are *not* enlightened is what keeps you from experiencing the infinite presence that is always here. When you are absolutely certain that enlightenment is always here, then everywhere you look, there it is: you can't avoid it.

So, what if *you* were to finally drop all of your notions . . . let go of all your ideas . . . relinquish all your judgements? What if *you* decided to discover what remains when all ideas of enlightenment, or not enlightenment, are stripped away?

I wonder what you would discover?

Enlightened awareness is the pristine presence that remains after all ideas have fallen away. It is your very essence, who you are and who you will always be.

You have always been enlightened. Just give up the belief that you are not, and just rest *as* what is. Do not question it. Do not quantify it. Don't touch it. Just be still in it.

Truth is. Peace is. Life is.

You are That.

✲ ✲ ✲

Over the years since that first stripping away, I came to realise that the subtracting, letting go, falling away, 'dying', is an ongoing, never-ending process. As identifications, resistances, tendencies, and mind games continue to be consumed by grace, the realisation of this boundless presence deepens. Purification is *still* happening –

it's just happening in the vaster context of grace: the grace of freedom.

Enlightenment is not a one-off experience, or a landing place, but an endless opening into the infinite.

In this ocean of love, I still enjoy singing, chanting, dancing, prayer, yoga, sitting for meditation – *not* because they will cause me to attain something called 'enlightenment', but just because bliss arises and my being enjoys it. I have no illusions that these activities will give me anything, but it is joyful to experience them nonetheless. I love singing and chanting – it opens up the heart. I adore sitting quietly in nature and meditation happens naturally, of its own accord. It's not something I do formally as a practice, it just arises as a pull from within, and the eyes close and I just rest.

The realisations continue to come: experiences of kundalini are endless. Awakenings and openings continue to happen. They all just arise in the vaster context of being.

And something deepens. Papaji gave me clear instructions that as I was resting in open awareness, unborn potential, I was not to take up residence as anything – especially not enlightenment, for that too is a trap.

Just be content to rest in this unknown, free from all labels, constructs and ideas.

Over the years, many people have asked me, 'Are you enlightened, Brandon?' I can only answer, 'I don't know'. In order to think about it, I would have to take up residence in some concept of enlightenment – as a some*body* who attained some*thing*. It all seems too effortful, and would only cause separation. I prefer not to rest as anything but pure awareness. I'm content to be in the unknown. Enlightenment already is: I don't need to take up residence as it. It's already shining everywhere.

So, you can relax in this vast unknown, and give up any ideas of enlightenment. It's not a landing place – just an endless opening into this infinite embrace.

Guided Introspection – Self-Inquiry

For this exercise, you might like to turn on the companion CD or you can just follow these simple instructions.

You are already free and completely whole. Your essence is vast and spacious, and the enlightened awareness you've been seeking is already present. It is calling you home to your self . . . right now.

There is nothing you can do to attain it, so just relax . . . for it is already here . . . it is who you are.

This simple process of self-inquiry is designed to penetrate the lies of who we *think* we are, and to open us into the truth of who we *really* are. It is a simple question, but it is the most powerful and profound one I know, for it can give you a direct experience of your infinite self, causing you to penetrate the labels you've come to identify yourself with.

In the beginning, your roles and labels may sometimes arise in response to the question. But if you continue to stay open and continue to inquire, eventually all the old identities will fall away and what will remain is unobscured awareness, freedom, your *Self*.

The experience of the Self most often arises as a word*less* response. It comes as a direct experience of vast spaciousness, of open stillness, of boundlessness.

Continue asking the question and allow it to pull you deeper into yourself.

Enlightened awareness is your own essence, and when all labels fall away, this pristine presence is all that remains.

So, find a quiet comfortable space to sit in for a few minutes.

You might like to take a few deep breaths in . . . and slowly exhale . . . Deep breath in . . . and slowly let it out . . . Slow breath in . . . and let it out.

Then, when you're ready, you may close your eyes, letting yourself become still and spacious . . . your awareness open spaciously in front . . . become vast behind . . . and infinite to all sides . . . boundless below . . . and spacious above.

And just rest as an ocean of awareness.

Innocently begin asking yourself, 'Who am I?' allowing whatever response arises to come up naturally . . . Open and again ask, 'Who am I?' still remaining open to directly experience the response rising from within.

Continue asking, 'Who am I? . . . Who am I *really*?' until all labels fall away . . . Then discover what remains – this ocean of

awareness. Then repeat the question . . . It will begin to carry you deeper into the boundlessness.

Continue asking until all is vast and spacious . . . and just rest . . . just soak . . . steep in your own presence . . . in the infinite ocean of your Self. And when you are ready you may open your eyes.

✲ ✲ ✲

Freedom *already* is
It's who you are, who you always will be
It's time to live in the freedom that is already here
It's time to live a life of Grace